Being a Sharefish in a Selfish World

"With great humor and insight, **Being a Sharefish in a Selfish World** takes readers on a lively journey of discovery, engaging them in an entertaining and profoundly significant exploration of the meaning of life and love, and our role in it all. Like that of Elizabeth Gilbert in **Eat, Pray, Love**, Oie Osterkamp's style is all at once smart, funny and highly relatable."

"From the very first page I was hooked and could not put the book down. I really think you're going to help God move mountains with this story!"

"The 'Immersion' chapter is one of the best images that I have ever read of how we interact with the Spirit of God."

"I've read two books recently that have made as big an impact on my life as anything I've ever read. William P. Young's **The Shack** dramatically changed the way I view my relationship with God, and **Being a Sharefish in a Selfish World** dramatically changed the way I view myself and my role in this world."

"A great read – a journey from being lost to finding oneself and the meaning of life."

"As I read the story, I literally felt as though I was absorbing it into the fabric of myself, and it immediately altered, in a very positive way, how I look at a number of things going on in my life."

"Mr. Osterkamp has a gift, both in this story God gave him and in the way He has empowered Mr. Osterkamp to put it together."

"I believe this story will be a powerful and far reaching messenger of God's goodness and desire for all of us."

"Thank you for writing **Being a Sharefish in a Selfish World.** Whenever I need to reminisce and recall those feelings of doing a huge service for someone and having a heart-felt and teary eyed response, it will only be a few page turns away."

"**Being a Sharefish in a Selfish World** was a perspective realignment experience for me. It reminded me that God, family, and friends need to be the priorities in our lives."

"**Being a Sharefish in a Selfish World** was a great reminder that God is always with us, especially in the most trying of times."

Phyllis Lightbourne

Being a Sharefish
in a
Selfish World

A novel by

Oie Osterkamp

Keep the Faith!

Oie

Being a Sharefish in a Selfish World

A novel by

Oie Osterkamp

Cover design by Metro Productions
www.metroproductions.com

Author photo by Jennifer Abbate Kanetzke
www.abbatestudios.com

Release 10/1/2008

International Standard Book Number - 1-4392-0859-X

Contents

Introduction

Water – plain, ordinary water – is one of the principal elements of life. The average adult body is composed of fifty-five to seventy percent water. Recently, our city experienced a serious, prolonged drought. Commercial and residential uses of water were rationed severely as the weatherman on television reported nightly on how many days worth of drinking water remained in the local reservoir which served as the source of our drinking supply. Businesses that used large amounts of water were forced to close and people reported neighbors who illegally watered their lawns to the local authorities.

On a global scale, some futurists predict that within the next century wars will be fought over drinkable water supplies. In the less hospitable climes of the world this has always been the case --- a deep, drinkable well is worth fighting for --- look it up in the Torah. Charitable organizations offer a chance to donate a well for a whole village. Recently, a community in a poor, mountainous area of the world was able to cut its infant mortality rate in half when they secured a clean drinking supply. When you get right down to it, we are as dependent on water as fish.

Fish can't just live in any old water. Their water must contain enough oxygen and nutrients to sustain their lives, and be free of toxins and organisms which would poison them. If the oxygen levels are depleted, or if the water becomes severely contaminated, the fish will die. In short, they must have "living" water. Their Creator lovingly provides them this living water in the lakes, streams and seas where they naturally thrive. Some fish are confined by other creatures to live in bowls or tanks (where their aquatic environment must be scrupulously maintained and regulated); but as any child who has seen a certain animated movie about fish can tell you; they would, if they could choose, swim in the "living" water for which they are designed.

We, too, are created to thrive in "living" water. If you don't believe it, just ask a Jewish man named Nicodemus, or a Samaritan woman at a well, and they will tell you. However, unlike fish, some of us choose to cut ourselves off from the "living" water which our Creator provides for us. Instead, we want to build our own sterile, artificial tank environments, with glass walls that allow us to look out without having to share our precious water with others who might be different, or even dangerous. Instead of sharing our natural environment, we focus our attention inward to insure that we can survive in our artificial environments, where those **others** can't get to us.

This book, written by my friend, Oie, is an invitation to leave our lonely tank water to swim in the deep, free waters for which we were created; and to there experience fellowship with our brothers and sisters and the Creator of us all. If you don't know about "living" water, this book can teach you to swim free. If you once swam in "living" water but traded it for a sterile tank, here are directions to the pathway home.

--- Stephen Brown

Foreward

A woman goes to the grocery store with her three children like she has done hundreds of times before. As she waits in line to check out, she mentally scans her "to do" list for the rest of the day. Suddenly she is startled back to reality. An animated conversation has taken place between the customer in front of her and the cashier. The cashier is smiling from ear to ear. As the woman with the three children takes her groceries out of her cart and sets them in front of the cashier, she asks the cashier what the conversation was about. The cashier tells her that the most unbelievable thing just happened. Her customer had asked her what her favorite candy bar was. When the cashier told her, the customer had reached over and gotten one of the bars, paid for it and handed it to the cashier. The customer smiled and told her that it was for her. The cashier said that she had worked at that store for years and nothing like that had ever happened before. Her wide smile accentuates her surprise and excitement.

The world is a much more beautiful and incredible place than you think, and each of us has a great deal of power to make it more so. Every day, all over the world millions of ordinary people are doing extraordinary things to make lives better for others (perhaps with a candy bar!). We usually won't recognize them until we learn to think like a sharefish. Then we begin to see them every day.

The story you are about to experience is a fictional story with a non-fictional point. For those non-literary folks, that normally means that even though the characters may not be real people, their experiences are very real. They are events that we all have experienced to some extent; or at least we have known people who have. The challenge we face is to learn from these experiences and grow from them.

The historical and Biblical data in the story is from reliable sources, although I have yet to find much about history that has not been questioned by some "expert" at some point. If you read something you do not understand or do not agree with, do your own research. It will be good for you. The point of the story, however, is the most reliable thing in the world, and whether you are young or old you can benefit from it immediately. What happened at the grocery store *was* real, and that small act changed adults' *and* children's worlds that day.

The point is very simple yet most of us find it difficult to adopt. We need each other. We are made to love and help one another. We need to stop talking about how we need to do better and get to the place where we actually do it. As you will see, sometimes it takes a new friend and 3,000 miles to help us get there.

At the end of your journey through this book, my prayer is for you to take just one thing that warmed your heart or ignited your spiritual flame or cleared the cobwebs from your faith,

…and become a sharefish.

To my wonderful wife, Becky,
a shining example of a sharefish

and

to our remarkable child, Oren.
Son, this story was written for you -
(I hope you don't mind if I share
it with a few other folks).

Chapter 1

Everyone Is Going Somewhere

"I can take you almost the whole way to where you're looking to go," he said with a grin. It took a minute for me to realize he was talking to me. I looked at my watch and was startled to find I had been staring at this last cup of coffee for twenty minutes.

My last ride had dropped me off at the diner somewhere in Otis, Oregon about three cups of coffee and two huge pieces of warm fresh peach pie earlier. The waitress noticed I wasn't a regular and had asked the usual "Where ya from? Where ya goin'?" questions when she came by with a refill. I didn't really feel like talking about it, but I needed a lift so I kept it short. "Trying to hitch a ride to North Carolina" seemed to satisfy her, even though she gave me a "You're about as far away as you can get" look. I was heading home...actually I was heading as far away as I could get from the West Coast. Too many wounds. Too many memories. The "West Coast" had kicked me out of her house for things that I had done, had not done, had forgotten to do, and honestly, probably would do. I was on the emotional edge and decided that distance gave me the best chance at keeping any semblance of sanity. "History repeating itself," I thought, shaking my head at myself in a mixture of disappointment and disgust.

"Is that all you got?" the man with the bright smile asked as he pointed to my tattered canvas duffle bag in the seat on the other side of the table. I figured it was his way of saying that if I wanted a ride, it was time to go so I nodded and grabbed the bag. "See you sometime soon, Ruby," the man said to the waitress. "Have a good trip, Izzy," the waitress grinned back, lifting her coffee pot like she was giving him a toast.

The man took my bag and stuck it behind the driver's seat of his rig. The truck looked as though it had seen the way from the West Coast to the East Coast several times. The red paint was faded and the name across the grill read "Int rnat nal." I chuckled to myself as I thought, "I'll buy three vowels, please!" I climbed in and discovered it was warm and comfortable inside. I was relieved to learn that the rumble I had heard earlier was not just in my head but was the diesel engine idling while we were in the diner. The man jumped into the driver's seat with the familiarity of years of practice and strapped himself in.

"Name's Isaac, but my friends call me Izzy." His eyes danced as he reached his hand across to shake mine. He didn't seem to mind that I didn't tell him my name. I didn't feel like I really had one at the moment. I silently wondered what he had to be so happy about. His face was kind, but showed the signs of someone who had worked hard outside for most of his life. Though tall and lean, he looked solid, like he had enjoyed his own share of peach pie at diners through the years. His clothes spoke of comfort instead of fashion. He looked to be in his mid fifties, but his eyes belied his age. They had the green hue of new maple leaves in spring mixed with amber and gold, like the colors of a wheat field blowing in a breeze. They were clear and bright, conveying a sense of sincerity and strength.

The truck took off and headed down Highway 18. We snaked through the beautiful Oregon countryside. Countless shades of green reflected the waning fall daylight as the trees waved me well wishes. It was like they knew I was not coming back. As we passed over hills and through valleys I reminisced about the hikes and wonderful vistas I had experienced during my two years there. Thanks to the constant hum of the engine and a belly full of pie I closed my eyes and didn't open them again until a dreamless four hours later.

"Where are we?" I asked.

"He speaks! He's alive!" Izzy grinned. "Well, my friend, we are farther than you know and closer than you think." I had no idea then just how profound that statement was.

I didn't know if it was the sleep or the distance, but my heart felt lighter, my growling stomach indicated it was empty, and my bladder informed me that *it* was full. Somehow sensing all this, Izzy pulled over at a restaurant that looked like it had been closed for years except for the two trucks and three cars in the parking lot. "You mind if we get a bite to eat?" Izzy winked at me.

The menu revealed that we were someplace in the Cascade Mountains halfway across Oregon on the Columbia River that marks the border with Washington. In another month or so there would be enough snow here to make traveling much more difficult. "At least I'm getting out in time," I told myself. That was enough information for me and I dug into a steaming slab of meatloaf that reminded me of grandmother's.

I ate more than I had eaten in weeks while Izzy caught up on the latest news with the folks behind the counter. I got up to pay and Izzy caught my eye. "It's handled, my friend. The next one's yours." His eyes were alive and honest, and the wrinkles that surrounded them deepened when he smiled.

Since I had no idea how long it would be until the next stop, I detoured into the restroom on the way out. When I looked at the reflection in the mirror, I grimaced. I looked awful. I needed a haircut. I needed a shave. I needed a shower. I looked like I had been homeless for much longer than a few days. I couldn't believe a thirty-four year old man could look so old. I couldn't help but shake my head in amazement that I had been offered a ride by anyone at all.

As we jumped back into the truck, I reached over and shook Izzy's hand. "Thanks for the meal. My name's Nyles."

"You're welcome, Nyles."

I couldn't explain it, but when he shook my hand it was as familiar as the feel of my old childhood baseball glove. I passed it off as emotional imbalance and settled in for the next section of the trip.

After what seemed like hours of rolling through the Rocky Mountains, I may have felt a little too comfortable with the situation and before I knew it I blurted out, "Aren't you curious about why I'm heading east?"

Izzy kept staring forward and eventually replied, "Everyone is heading somewhere, Nyles. They have to. Some do it on the road. Some do it inside themselves. Either running from something or toward something. Sometimes they don't know which. Some find what they're looking for, others think they find it a few times before they actually do and sadly some folks don't find it at all." A sense of familiarity hit me again. I quickly dismissed it as the song "I Still Haven't Found What I'm Looking For" played in my head, competing with the country and western music that murmured through the static of the dashboard speakers.

"I guess I'm doing both," I said. "I'm running from something and toward something. I think I know what I'm running from, but I'm not sure what I'm running to." I know Izzy was just trying to make conversation, and I tried to be congenial. After all, he was my ticket east. It seemed that with every question my answer sounded contrived while inside my heart was screaming "Liar, liar!" Izzy asked about my occupation. I told him I was a carpenter at a boat building company. My mind protested with the real story of how I would miss days due to long nights of partying and just plain irresponsibility. He asked about my family life, and while I told him a whitewashed tale of how I had just ended a relationship, my conscience bellowed in my head about how I had messed up a good thing by being untrustworthy and she had kicked me out. My head began to throb and I finally acted like I was asleep to try and quiet the demons.

Reflecting on my life's mistakes made hundreds of miles of highway through the mountains passing under our wheels seem timeless. Izzy didn't say much as we rolled through Idaho, Utah, and most of Wyoming. Or if he did, I didn't hear him. My emotions spewed through my mind like molten lava. Every time I thought I was finished, my heart would heave and more skeletons would come out to reintroduce themselves and confirm why I felt useless and worthless. The only pauses came with meals and sleep. Finally, it was as though the mountains knew when I was through, because when I finished reviewing the horrible film that was my life, the twists and turns and ups and downs of the mountain roads stopped and the plains lay flat before us. It was as if a giant steam roller had lumbered through, flattening everything in its path. As I put an emotional period at the end of my last thought, I was seized with an inexplicable fear that Izzy was going to pull over and kick me out. I tried to secure my one and only way to the east by firmly planting a seed of sympathy. I thanked Izzy for the ride as I carefully stitched a story of seventy percent truth and thirty percent fabrication that detailed how I had been kicked out of the house and fired from my job.

To gauge his response, I sent up a test balloon. "So, I guess I got what I deserved, huh." I'm not sure how long it took for Izzy to answer me. I was busy swimming through the conflicting feelings of guilt my stories had resurrected and peace that my purging had induced.

Izzy breathed deeply like he wanted to say something yet didn't know exactly how to put it. He turned to me slowly, caught my eyes with his, and turned back to the road. "Depends on what you do next." he said. "My dad used to tell me that there are times in life that can be a mess. Then he'd look at me and ask if I knew what a mess was. Even though I knew what he was going to say, I'd always say 'no.' He'd grin and say that a mess was twenty pounds of manure in a ten pound bag. He'd laugh and laugh. Then he'd tell me how some folks would think they had ruined their shoes forever when they'd stepped in it and other folks had made a mighty good living selling it to folks as fertilizer. He'd look at me and tell me everybody stepped in it at some point. Good folks learn from it and move on. Smart folks saw where other folks had stepped in it and avoided stepping in that pile, even though there were always more piles to look out for. Wise folks learn from others' mistakes and use it to make their lives better. The main point is, Nyles, is that everybody steps in it."

Finally confident that Izzy wasn't going to kick me out and realizing I had been so self-absorbed since I met him that I knew nothing but his first name, I casually asked him, "What about you, Izzy? Are you running to or running from?"

I could sense his hands tighten around the steering wheel a bit as if the road ahead might be a bit more of a challenge to negotiate. He calmly replied, "I know misery loves company but it hates competition." He turned and forced a wink. "If you really want to know, I'll tell you, under one condition." I nodded. "You can stop me any time you think you've heard enough, or too much, for that matter. You good with that?" By reflex I swallowed, and nodded slowly.

I had no idea the next few days would change my life forever.

Chapter 2

Scene One; Scene Two

"Let me start by giving you two scenarios and we'll go from there, OK?" Izzy looked toward me with eyebrows raised to emphasize the question mark. After I nodded my approval, he took a deep breath, stared out through his bug-splattered windshield, and began to speak as we cruised down the highway that was so straight and long through the miles of corn that it narrowed to a point and disappeared in the horizon.

"Scene one. It's March and a man stands on the stage in Albuquerque, New Mexico, excited and overwhelmed. He looks out over the crowd and sees a huge auditorium full of executives from companies all over the country hoping to be named one of the *Inc. 500 Magazine's* fastest growing companies for that year. When the publisher of *Inc.* calls his name, the man numbly reaches over, shakes the publisher's hand and accepts a glass encased cover of the magazine as he is introduced as an owner of the seventh fastest growing privately owned company in the United States over the past five years. The crowd of executives stands as they applaud. The man's mind reels as he recalls the experience of starting the company with one truck, two friends and an idea. Now, here he was, 500 trucks and dozens of employees later. What a ride it had been.

"Later that evening he stares at the ceiling of his hotel room through the early morning hours, wondering just how far he could take this company. When he returns from his trip, magazines and other media clamor for interviews to find out the secret of his success. He is even asked for his autograph at a restaurant from a man who has read an article about him while on a flight one day earlier. To top it off, his wife and her work partner capped a five year successful run at selling software for a national company by winning the sales team of the year for the entire country. To anyone looking at his life from the outside, life was good.

"Now, scene two. The man stares blankly at the wall of his office noticing how the paint has faded where the awards and artwork used to hang. His desk has dust marks identifying where the computer, his stapler and picture frames once sat. The cardboard box of pictures and desk items sits at an angle in the doorway like a sentry. He keeps reliving the series of events that led to this moment.

"The company had gone out of business due to a national fraud ring that had drained the company's finances and pillaged their cash position. It happened so quickly they could not respond fast enough. He and his partners had spent the last few months scrambling to make sure their employees found new jobs and their clients would be serviced in their absence. He was left with nothing but the box of mementos and motivational posters.

"At home, the man's wife had delivered news that completely decimated his heart. His marriage had evaporated. Years of marriage. Poof. Gone. Years of sweat in the entrepreneurial game. Poof. Gone. He is shaken to his very core. To paraphrase a popular business analogy, his onion had been completely peeled.

"His eye catches something sticking out of the box in the doorway. Tears fill his eyes as he recognizes the coffee cup with *Inc. 500* etched on the side. It is stuck in the corner of the box. The round cup in the square hole. He fights the urge to smash it against the blank wall.

"Two scenes. Same man. Me. Two scenes. Six months apart. Six months that in some ways seemed like six seconds and in

25

others like six lifetimes. In six months I went from sharing a beautiful home on the golf course with my beautiful wife to a lonely room in a friend's house with all my belongings in a metal storage unit. As God has a tendency to teach us, however, the good was not as good as it looked and the bad revealed some very good things."

I interrupted Izzy right there. "That's terrible that you had to go through all that, but please don't give me a song and dance about God. I gave up on God a long time ago," I said with disgust as I looked out my window at the night sky.

Izzy countered with a chuckle. "That's OK, Nyles. God didn't give up on you. Do you want me to keep going?"

Not knowing if he meant he was going to stop in the middle of nowhere and let me out, I figured I could endure a little more. In fact, I was curious as to how someone with such bad luck now seemed to be so happy. Had he won the lottery? "Idiot," I answered myself. "He drives a truck." Okay then, what? After shaking my head at myself for carrying on a conversation in my head, I turned to Izzy. "So you were married before?" I asked. "What happened?"

Izzy's eyes softened. He took a deep breath and began. "She was beautiful. The only thing that was more beautiful than her looks was her heart. She was just a good person through and through. I was sure I had found my life mate. We had a lot of fun together. The future looked bright. Then one day things changed."

Izzy became quiet and stared out through the windshield for what seemed like half an hour. Just as I was about to ask him if he was all right, he began to speak as if talking to himself.

Chapter 3

Survival Mode

"Please help me," Izzy said softly. I was getting ready to ask him what kind of help he needed when he cleared his throat and continued his story.

"Those words and the fear in her eyes will haunt me forever. It was the week after our first Thanksgiving together as a married couple. Her two sisters were visiting us for a few days to help us decorate for Christmas. The tree stood bare in its stand in the bay window of our living room. The wonderful aroma of Christmas tea filtered through the house as it simmered in the kitchen. Boxes of ornaments resembling stacks of large building blocks sat in piles around the fireplace, competing for our attention to be the first one opened for decorating the tree. We waited for my wife to come downstairs to begin the decorating. She had said she was not feeling well earlier and had gone upstairs to get some rest. After waiting for over an hour, I went upstairs to see how she was feeling.

"Her skin was the color of snow right before it melts away, that unhealthy gray that darkened as it closed in on her eyes. Oh my dear, her eyes, normally dancing with life, were wide with fear as if she was keeping company with a gang of demons. She grabbed my hand as I sat on the bed beside her. 'Please help me,' she pleaded.

" 'What's wrong?' I asked her. 'Is there anything I can get for you?'

"All she said was, 'Please help me.' A lone tear escaped the corner of her eye and rolled down the side of her face. In a split second I went from mildly worried to very concerned.

"I commanded her to tell me what was going on.

"She brought her other hand from underneath the covers and handed me a note and an empty prescription bottle. The note was a suicide note. The bottle was supposed to be full of anti-depressants. I scooped her up and ran to my car. Her limp body felt like a long bag of laundry. I prayed as I violated every traffic law in the city getting her to the emergency room. I handed her and the bottle to someone in green scrubs who whisked her behind two swinging doors barking orders like a commander on a battlefield. As I watched the doors slowly stop swinging and come to a stop, hoping someone was going to come bursting back through them to tell me this was all just a bad dream, I realized that I had not said anything to her sisters when I left.

"I could not bring myself to tell them the truth when I called them. Riding the wonderful white lie train I told them that she was very sick and that the doctors were evaluating her. I told them that I would call them back when I knew something and to stay at the house, knowing full well that they would soon be on their way to the emergency room. Even though I wanted to be alone to clear my head I figured the white lie train would fly off the tracks if I told them the wrong hospital, so I told them where I was. Then I began my own evaluation. What if she died and I never knew why she did this? I suddenly remembered the note. I reached in my coat pocket and slowly unfolded it like it might explode in my face.

"The words began to swim off of the page and jump out of the sentences. *Depressed, father, abuse, undeserving, sorry, so sorry, pain, relief, forgiveness.* My emotions jumped at me like a Whack-a-Mole game. Anger, denial, love, compassion, anger, love, betrayal, concern, denial. I sat down sullenly in one of those well-worn orange plastic chairs that are attached in rows of five that lined the wall. The emergency room was packed with sick people and families, yet I never felt so alone and so helpless. The tears began.

"I heard my name and looked up wondering how the doctor knew my first name, but it was her sisters. I didn't have the strength to lie so I told them all I knew and handed over the note. We all just sat there. I mean, what do you say when you have so many questions with no answers? I tried to pray with little success. I was just as angry with God as I was with the situation. I had just as many questions for Him as I did for her. The weight of my loneliness felt like a thick moldy blanket over my face that made it extremely difficult for me to breathe.

"Another person in green scrubs came up to us. She had black marks all over her front like someone had thrown old ashes out of a grill onto her. 'Someone was watching over your wife tonight, sir,' she began. 'Another three minutes and we might have lost her.' She led me through the double doors into a small cubicle surrounded by white curtains that had taken the brunt of the grill ashes. In the middle of a large splatter of black ash, I saw a woman who looked a little like my wife sleeping peacefully with several tubes sticking out of her arms, nose, mouth and some places that remained under the covers. Her breaths were fast and shallow, like she was blowing birthday candles out one at a time. Reading my mind, the girl in the green scrubs explained that they had forced charcoal down my wife's throat to make her vomit the pills before they dissolved completely. Now all we could do was wait. Scrubs lady told me that in the best-case scenario my wife was not going to be coherent for at least twelve hours so I should get some rest. She put her hands on my shoulders and looked me in the eye. 'I mean it. Get some rest. You are going to need your strength when she wakes up.'

"My legs wobbled as I unsteadily trudged out in the hallway to fill in the family. Night turned into day as we sat in the hospital coffee shop and talked. I was fortunate to have these two young women sitting there with me. One of my wife's sisters, a wonderful person with a passion for nature, had a master's degree in social work and counseled troubled youth. Perfect. I was feeling pretty troubled. My wife's other sister was also a phenomenal person and was in school getting her degree in Christian counseling. Excellent. My Christianity was pretty shaky. For the next twelve hours, I was their patient. I'm not sure I would have made it without them.

"The next few weeks were spent in rehab centers, psychiatrists' offices, and staring at the ceiling over the couch in the living room trying to make sense of what went on in the rehab centers and psychiatrists' offices. I could not make myself believe some of the things I was hearing – from her, her family, and from her doctors. It was like I went to sleep and woke up in a strange land where people I thought I knew were speaking a foreign language I could not comprehend. I realized that the evil claws of denial were deeply embedded in me. Over time, I was able to force the damaging emotions aside and let mature emotions prevail. The focus was on getting her better and home. My feelings could be dealt with later. I went into what I call 'survival mode'."

Chapter 4

Crumbling Facade

Izzy took a long drink from his bottle of water and continued. "When I could finally see her, I remained strong as she apologized profusely and gave me a wonderful heartfelt letter that she had written in the hospital that promised she would never try to leave me again. As I slipped it in my pocket I felt the other letter. I had brought it with me to ask her about some of the things she had written. I decided to wait. I still have both letters.

"Things went quite well for about a year. Then I pulled into our driveway one day after work and her car was there. She usually went to the gym after work so it kind of surprised me. As soon as I opened the door I knew something was terribly wrong. I called her name. Nothing. I ran upstairs and saw her lying on the bathroom floor. I thought she was gone. I called 911 and the paramedics took her away pumping air in her lungs with a large green bag.

"Too late for the charcoal, they gave her something to counteract the pills she had taken. They told me to pray and wait. She began screaming about 4:00 a.m. which made me leap with joy even though she was hallucinating about bugs crawling all over the walls. I held her tightly. She was going to make it. I went back into survival mode.

"We talked through her abuse again with some added episodes that she had begun to remember. When the memories had gotten too bad, she had started pulling the capsules of her pills apart and dumping the medicine in an empty prescription bottle. She had driven around in her car for two weeks with a prescription bottle almost a quarter full of pure medicine rolling around under the driver's seat. We had been in that car together. We had laughed in that car together. Just the night prior to the attempt, we had another couple over for dinner and had a great time. Once again, no one around her had a clue. Not me. Not her family. Not her doctors.

"Another two weeks in rehab. More psychiatrists. More medications.

"For the next twenty years, the little things that people take for granted every day gave me a little jolt in my gut like a paper cut. I would pull in my driveway, take a deep breath, and open the front door not knowing what I would find even if I had just talked to her before leaving the office. The receptionist at work would buzz me and let me know she was on the line and I would hesitate for a fraction of a second before I picked up.

"Why? There were five more attempts in those years. No need to go into details. Each one perilously close to being 'the one.' Each one brought on by more memories of pain and abuse. Each ending with a promise of it never happening again. There were periods of depression where she could not get out of bed for weeks. The day she and her partner won the national sales award, she was balled up in a chair in our living room, unable to go to the celebration in Denver. There was a period where she would inexplicably beg to go see a movie every day for 22 straight days. There were days when I would take her to work with me because she didn't want to be alone. There were days she would not talk to me because she wanted to be alone. The demon of depression had set up housekeeping in her soul and had a firm grip…on both of us.

"I vowed to be the one thing in her life that she could count on. I had sworn before God and our families and friends that 'until death us do part.' No matter how close we had been, I was going to be her rock. I knew what happened to her as a child wasn't her fault. At some point in those years, we became more friends than a married couple. I understood that. A close physical relationship is extremely difficult when bad childhood memories are tied to it. I kind of laughed to myself sometimes that it was punishment for all my cavorting when I was younger. We got used to it after awhile. In the weeks and months between attempts we had some really great times. We loved each other. We cared for each other. We did all the things happy couples do. We had wonderful friends. We were faithful church members. We both had successful careers. We both had the secret.

"The secret? That's right. Through all the attempts and corresponding treatment, only a select number of family, inner circle friends, and medical professionals knew what was going on. She was from a small town. Her mother was concerned about any embarrassment it could cause to the family. To the world at large it looked like we had it made. The perfect couple.

"Then it happened. The façade began to crumble. While she was in the treatment center after her fifth attempt I met with her doctors. They began to explore the codependent side of her depression with me. I was so intent on making her life as easy as possible when she was feeling good it was possible that I was actually making it more difficult for her to get to the 'tipping point' of recovery. After much thought and prayer I called our inner circle and planned a meeting for everyone to get together. I could only get through this once.

"I thanked the group for all of their support and friendship through the years. I told them that I had made a decision that would require them to be even more supportive. Through help from her counselors I had realized that she would always get better with me by her side, but she may never get 'well.' My own health was suffering. The company that I had started seven years earlier had been defrauded, our bank abandoned us, and I had spent the last few months in negotiations determining whether or not I had to file bankruptcy. With the support of a few outstanding friends and a company that agreed to continue service to all our customers and hire all our employees, I was able to avert bankruptcy by a few hundred dollars. Looking bankruptcy in the face, I felt an incredibly heavy burden. I had no respite at home. I had no respite at work. I was running on fumes.

"I had taken a stress test that asked several questions about life events that cause harmful stress. A score of less than 50 meant that you were very 'stress-healthy.' A score of over 200 meant that you were in the danger zone and that 'disease was imminent' and suggested immediate professional attention. My score was 325. A short-term separation from me after she was released from the hospital may be just what she needed to jump start her recovery and give me much needed rest and recovery of my own.

"It lasted two months. I got a call early one afternoon from a friend of hers where she was staying down at the beach. Her friend had left for work that day and noticed that my wife's car was gone. When she came home for lunch the car was still gone. She tried to call my wife's cell phone. She heard a ring behind the closed bedroom door. She knocked. No answer. When she opened the door she saw an open pocketbook, a wallet, a cell phone and no keys. She called me and frantically explained the situation.

"I headed for the coast. Her friend and I talked several times via phone on the way down. We figured she could have been gone for over twelve hours. The police searched. The Coast Guard searched. I searched every cottage and side street for miles looking for her car. I finally got a call about seven o'clock that evening that she had been found behind an electrical substation in a neighborhood close to her friend's neighborhood. She was barely breathing and was totally incoherent. She would not open her door. I used my key and got her out as the ambulance drove up.

"If she had nine lives she had used up life number six. After another long night in the hospital, the doctor recommended one of the best treatment hospitals for depression and abuse patients in the Southeast. The only caveat was that it was not a voluntary admittance facility. That meant that to get her into this facility, I would have to give the psychiatrist permission to involuntarily commit her. I could not take her. The sheriff had to handcuff her and take her. Staring at the back of her head in the back seat of that sheriff's car during the two-hour drive was one of the most difficult things I've ever endured."

Chapter 5

Secrets and Sacrifices

"The facility was wonderful. I saw some improvement in each visit. Then one rainy Saturday morning I went into an improvised visiting area (a table and two chairs in the middle of a gymnasium) and waited. After about thirty minutes she came walking in, her eyes red from crying. There was something she needed to tell me, she whimpered. I thought to myself what in the world could be worse than what we had been through over the years. She slowly raised her face to me. 'My family has always been about secrets,' she began. 'I have one too.' I told her not to worry. Just tell me.

"She told me of an affair she had with one of our dear friends for a year and a half. Her words echoed in my head. It could have been because the room was so big, but all of a sudden I felt very small. I'm not sure of much else after that. I hugged her and told her to continue to get better and I got on the highway.

"After about a mile I took an exit on a rural road, pulled over and vomited. I could feel my heart exploding like a crystal dish being dropped on a marble floor.

"As the miles passed by, my rage grew. It was as if each of the white stripes on the highway added an exclamation point at the end of my fits of anger as they passed under my car. The only thing that kept me safe on the road was cruise control. My feet were stomping. My hands were banging. My screams were wiped from the inside of the windshield by the constant drone of the wiper blades as it began to rain harder and harder.

"Exhausted as I pulled in the driveway, I barely made it in the house before I passed out on the couch. I woke up with a sore throat, crusty eyes, and a headache that pounded with every breath I took.

"I literally had no idea what to do next. Use whatever metaphor you wish. My sails had no wind. My well was dry. My cupboard was empty. I was a shell of a man.

"The decisions I made over the next few weeks were sound ones and I stand by them. The way I carried out those decisions, however, was less than stellar. I sure would love a couple of do-over's. It would probably have done a world of good for me to spend a couple of weeks in one of those recovery facilities myself. Totally exhausted, on the verge of breakdown, full of anger, I was in no shape to be making and carrying out decisions of any kind.

"I stewed for a while, talked to some friends and trusted associates, and filed for divorce. I realized that it was one thing to sacrifice for someone you love; it was another thing entirely to be sacrificed by them.

"For those who do not believe in divorce, I respect that. It's awful. Even when you know in the deepest part of your soul it's the right thing to do, it's still awful. Anyway, there I was. Lowest of the low. Defeated. Disheartened.

"Alone.

"Or so I thought."

Chapter 6

Something Bigger Than Me

Izzy stopped talking and stared out the windshield for what seemed like ten minutes. "Well?" I asked him. Izzy pulled into the parking lot of yet another out of the way diner somewhere around Kansas City that looked like it had long been forgotten by everyone but Izzy and a couple of regulars.

"I need to refuel," Izzy winked as he patted his belly and headed into the diner although I noted that his shoulders seemed to slump a little as he lumbered across the parking lot. I spent the meal recounting his heart wrenching ordeal to myself and making mental notes of questions I wanted to ask him, if given the opportunity. I relived the selfish way I had been treating my own relationships with women and even my family. I fought the guilt that was creeping into my soul when I compared how I had whined about how bad I had it to how strong Izzy seemed after his experiences. I wanted to know how he did it.

Izzy spent the time talking and laughing with the small entourage of regulars at the booth in the corner of the restaurant. When we were finished, we waved goodbye and headed back to the truck. I noticed he was walking straight again and with purpose. About halfway, Izzy stopped and turned to me.

"You may not want to hear the next part of the story," Izzy said as his eyes twinkled. "It's got some God in it."

I smiled back. "I didn't say I didn't *believe* in God," I confessed. "I just said I had given up on him." He patted me on the back and headed for the truck. I looked around and realized that I had no earthly idea where I was. The strange thing about it, though, was that I had a warm feeling of total comfort with that. I shook my head at myself and hopped in the truck. To my dismay, Izzy did not immediately continue his story. He talked a little about how beautiful our country is and how people should get out and see it more. Then he just stared out through the windshield and hummed along with the radio. He told a few stories of people he had met on the road and how true friendships do not have boundaries of space and time. It was driving me crazy.

To prime the story pump, I coaxed, "I'm really sorry all that happened to you, Izzy. I know what it is like to lose someone you love but not in the way you did, and I don't know what it is like to lose your business. I especially don't know what it is like to lose both at the same time. If that had happened to me I'm not sure I would have made it. So... I guess you still had this truck and decided to go back on the road and start all over again, right?"

"Eventually," Izzy replied. "There were a few things that I had to go through first. I sat around and felt sorry for myself for a while. I had started painting some years earlier so I spent a lot of time doing that. As my heart began to heal, I began to meet some people that changed me into what I am today. God began to send me sharefish."

I almost choked on my coffee. "Whatfish? What the heck's a sharefish?" I asked Izzy.

Izzy cocked his head back and gave a hearty laugh. "I knew that would get you! You see, one of the things I figured out was that I was spending a lot of time thinking about _me_. In my efforts to heal, I concentrated on what I could do for *me* and what I expected others to do for *me*, including God. I tricked myself into thinking I was looking for my purpose in life. What I was actually doing was limiting myself by just including myself.

"One day it hit me: I needed something *bigger* than me. I had read about people who have found their 'calling' and spend their lives fulfilling it. I had read about people who have overcome incredible odds and incredible loss and incredible pain to do some amazing things. It was all very interesting and in some cases, inspiring, but it kind of left me empty as well.

"You see, I'm just an average guy. Not average in a mediocre way, just average. In fact, I grew up in North Carolina just like you, Nyles. I've had my share of joys and pains, yet if you placed me on the bell curve of human existence I'm sure I would be around the middle of the curve. Don't get me wrong. I don't want to trade five years of my life for five years in a concentration camp in Southern Borneo, nor would I have wanted to be on the 97th floor of the World Trade Center on that fateful September 11th. I do not have any regret that I was not born with the predisposition to be an international spy wanting my martinis 'shaken, not stirred,' and I don't wish that I was born into great wealth.

"Honestly, I have always just wanted to find that thing, that one thing, that fills my heart with passion and will keep me up at night in anticipation of how I can take it to the next level. That 'thing' that some people are born with, like the famous concert

50

pianist who was told after an outstanding performance, 'I would give my life to play like that.' He calmly replied, 'I did.' "

Izzy could tell I was getting ready to interrupt him to ask about the sharefish thing. He chuckled as he continued. "Now, I'm not complaining. I am now married to an amazing woman who loves me dearly and says I am the answer to her lifelong prayers. We have a home, we have a family, I have a job, I have friends I would not trade for anything. My family has always loved and supported me with no questions asked. I am normally able to choose what I have for supper, which puts me in the 20% of people in the world who can do the same. This isn't about that.

"Perhaps it is something in all of us that remains unsettled. Something that keeps us squinting at the horizon. A big question mark in the pit of our stomachs. 'Is this what it's all about? Am I doing what God wants me to do? Should I be more thankful and less anxious?' Yet I continued to poke the fire of my life looking for the ember that would ignite into a burning passion that guides my heart into a glow for the world to see."

Izzy looked at me quickly and smiled. "I needed something bigger than me."

Izzy let the "something bigger than me" swim around in my head for a few miles. As I was getting ready to ask him what he meant by that statement, he answered it for me.

"I had experienced glimpses of this throughout my life, like smelling the popcorn but not being allowed to put my hand in the bowl. There had been times when I knew I was in the right place at the right time doing the right thing for the right reason. I mean a bigger than me place at a bigger than me time doing a bigger than me thing for a bigger than me reason. That's why I knew I didn't have it when I didn't have it. I wondered sometimes if it was just me.

"When I started being a sharefish I learned that having something bigger than me doesn't mean what the ads on TV and in magazines tell me. It's not about stuff. It's not about anything you can buy. It's too valuable for that. It's not about how your body looks or what kind of clothes you wear or what kind of car you drive or any of that stuff. It's not about hip-hop or 'the hood' or the corporate game or 'he with the most toys wins.' It's not about gender, ethnicity, religion, or creed. These are all things that people have made into measuring sticks that keep us focused on where we stand in relation to each other instead of *relating to* each other.

"Take a minute and think about all the information that hits you on a daily basis. What you read, what you hear, what you watch, who you spend time with, all of it. I did. Here's what I realized. We live in a selfish world. A 'self-ish' world. We have gone from *Life* magazine to *Self* magazine. I didn't want to live in a selfish world.

"I wanted to have a life that is bigger than me. Not bigger than you. Bigger than me. God could not fill me with his love as long as I was full of myself. I wanted to grow in faith and in spirit. I wanted to make life better for someone I haven't met. I wanted the world to be better because I spent some time here. I wanted God to hug me and look me in the eyes when I finally get to Him and say to me, 'Well done, my good and faithful servant.'

"I wanted to move from living in a **selfish** world to living in a **sharefish** world. I prayed that I could learn how to change my life to one that was bigger than me. A sharefish life. It was only a prayer away. People began to show up in my daily walk that exemplified this sharefish principle. Would you like to hear about some of these folks?"

"Absolutely!" I said curiously, trying to picture what a sharefish would look like. Izzy must have noticed the puzzled look on my face because he grinned from ear to ear and shook his head.

"I know," he began, "It was all new to me as well. It all started with John. John started out in a place that made him the ultimate selfish. Let me give you some background to help you understand John's journey."

Chapter 7

Addiction

Izzy scratched his chin and stared out the window thoughtfully as he decided exactly how he would begin John's story. About the time my mind began to wander, Izzy startled me with his strong voice. "His thoughts were controlled by it. He was possessed by it. He could not escape it. He begged. He pleaded. He would not be released from it.

"He fooled himself sometimes by thinking he could fight it by himself. He would make a plan and stick to it, he would promise himself. He would break that promise. Again. And again. And again.

"I met John when I owned my company. We needed one of our benefits plans to be customized and he was one of the best benefits attorneys in the state. He and I hit it off from the start. He made me feel comfortable immediately that we had made the right choice. We talked frequently over the weeks that the plan was put together. He did excellent work. We shook hands and as I left I remember thinking that if our company ever needed anything else, I would go to him first. We didn't, so I didn't.

"Fast-forward a couple of years. Our company had been defrauded and had imploded. I was out of work, my marriage was crushed, my heart was broken, and I was putting the pieces back together. I was bored. I was depressed. I was lonely. I spent most of my time feeling sorry for myself with a little painting thrown in to keep me from feeling totally pathetic.

"I decided that maybe I would do some volunteer work to help change the momentum of my life. I had heard some neat stuff about a facility called The Healing Home. I thought I would check it out. What a cool place! It felt clean and friendly. The director took me around and introduced me to the staff. These dedicated professionals looked me straight in the eyes with compassionate spirits that filled the room. They helped homeless and addicted men turn their lives around. I liked the concept. There were several phases of the program. It starts in the detox unit. From there the men go to living in a room with 24 men. If they earn it, they then move to a room with 12 men. If they earn it, they then move to a room with six men. If they earn it, they then move to a room with two men. If they earn it, they can claim their own private room. From there they begin to find somewhere outside of The Healing Home to live and work. There are no locks on the doors. The men can leave whenever they wish, although they may not be invited back. They may be asked to leave if the rules of respect are not followed. The men pretty much run the whole place. With guidance, they cook, they clean, they maintain, they train.

"Anyway, the director gave me the overview in his office and then began to give me the tour. I was incredibly impressed that there was such a place for the down and out. As we left the lobby area, the director said that even though he could talk for hours about the merits of the program, it would be much better coming from one of the actual guests. He then introduced me to my tour guide.

"As I turned to shake the hand of my new guide, my lungs nearly collapsed from my gasp and my mouth was open as wide as the mop bucket he was holding. It was John! It was really weird because *I* was the one who was embarrassed. He smiled widely and shook my hand vigorously and told me how good it was to see me. The next fifteen minutes or so are kind of gray as I tried to make sense of it all. Have you ever seen someone and knew you knew them but just couldn't place them? Then you realize where you knew them from and it all makes sense? Well, this was the opposite. I knew this person and the person I knew didn't belong here. I had always seen him dressed in expensive suits carrying a laptop computer. Here he was in a comfortable white shirt and khaki pants holding a mop and bucket. If something like this could happen to him, what in the world could happen to me? My head began to throb.

"We began our tour and headed through the courtyard. Finally, I stopped in the middle of the sidewalk between the cafeteria and the courtyard. I had to know what happened. John stopped mid-sentence and looked at me. I turned to John and didn't have to say a word. He smiled broadly and motioned toward one of the benches in the courtyard.

"He cleared his throat, and for the first time I noticed a bit of sadness in his eyes. 'I had nowhere else to turn,' he said slowly. He hesitated as he gathered his thoughts. It seemed like it took him an hour. 'I had it all, or so I thought,' he began. 'I was living the good life. I was making a lot of money. I was well respected in my field and in my firm. I provided a huge home for my wife and children. I also provided them with a living hell.'

"He began to confess the demons that had dug their nails into his very soul: cocaine, alcohol, women. He had struggled with these demons for a few years. He remembered the beginning of the downfall. His nine-year-old son had come home from school that day with a fever. Thirty days and ten operations later he was watching his son being lowered into a grave. As each shovel of earth was thrown on the casket, a piece of him began to be buried under the dirt as well. He started drinking to forget. He began to take drugs to feel normal. He began to pursue women in search of his manhood.

"Whenever he reached bottom, he reached out for help. He would enter a high-dollar rehab 'country club' that would patch him back together for a little while. His wife and remaining two children were there to support him. He would formulate a plan, and earnestly focus on that plan. Then the demon would stealthily emerge. He might be at a red light and glance over at the car next to him. His plan of sobriety and trust would self-destruct step by step. First, the attractive woman, then thirst, and then ache to guilt to lie to promise to lie to lie to lie until he found himself awakening in an unfamiliar place with an unfamiliar woman with a *very* familiar after effect. He had even lied to himself to the point that he had volunteered at The Healing Home during one of his sober times to 'prove' to himself that *this time* was going to be different.

"He was right. Only not in the way he thought. One day the demons took such a hold on John that he drove to the airport and booked a flight to the Bahamas for a week's vacation, telling himself that he had to 'get away.' Get away he did. When the fog lifted and the bottom was staring him in the face, three months of booze and drugs and women lay in his wake. He realized that his family had no idea where he was or for that matter if he still was alive. He had parked his luxury car in a twenty-four dollar a day parking space at the airport. He had not paid the mortgage and other bills for three months. His cell phone mailbox was full of messages from family and co-workers with escalating messages of concern and fear. John came home and went to the two places he felt safe, his wife's arms and The Healing Home.

"With the support of his family, John went from being a volunteer at The Healing Home to a resident. He stood in the lines, he went to the meetings, he did his chores…and he obsessed about his demons. The pull was fresh and strong. The lies were replaced with exciting memories. The pain was pushed aside by the intense and adventurous pleasure that awaited him on the outside. He went to his friend the director of The Healing Home and mapped out his plan. He told him that he needed to leave for a couple of weeks to 'get some things straightened out on the outside.' His family needed some stuff done. He needed to go by the office and talk with his partners. He needed to make sure his bills were caught up so his car and his house would not be repossessed.

"That's a great plan,' the director said. 'I have an idea. Why don't we hire someone to do those things for you? I know the perfect person. The veins in his arms don't work right any more because they've had too many needles injecting poison into them.

Eight out of ten decisions he has made in the past three years have been dangerous and devastating to him and to all who care about him. He can't even remember most of what he has done for the past three months. What do you think, John? Does he sound like a good hire to you?'

"John said that it was as if someone opened up a drain plug in the bottom of his feet and the demons slowly left his body, starting from the top of his head and inching down his body until he felt the last drop leave. His friend was exactly right. John finally began to see himself as he truly was, not as the lie. Healing finally had rich soil in which to grow. As he dropped, exhausted, in his cot that night, he thought about his entire earthly possessions that lived under his cot in the two plastic boxes. He smiled contentedly. For the first time he could remember, his life was about who he *was*, not what he had.

"The next day he took a walk on the grounds of an old hospital a mile or so from The Healing Home. There in the middle of a hilly grassy area was a lone maple tree. A large maple tree. A grandpa of a maple tree.

"As the sun shone brightly on the leaves and the breeze made them wave, a realization struck John. There *was* something bigger than him – call it God if you want to - that he needed to somehow connect with to make it through the next abyss. The warmth of the power of this feeling bathed him as he took in the inconceivable panorama before him. Later that evening he began to pray, but his demons tried to cast doubt on his prayers. Who was *he* to be talking to God, they taunted. What makes him think that of the millions of people who are praying right now, that God would pick *him* to listen to? John fought back. He concentrated from the depths of his soul. As he lay back on his cot and stared at the ceiling tiles, he fought the demons that fought to break his prayer by suggesting that he count the tiles. God help me, he whispered to himself. 'Hey John. Is that a new water spot?' the demons offered, their voices becoming fainter. The ceiling tiles began to disappear and John began to connect with heaven. His demons cowered and slinked back into oblivion until their next opportunity. He imagined a searchlight emanating from his heart through the ceiling tiles, through the roof, higher still, through the trees, higher, higher, through the clouds, out of the earth's atmosphere, higher, higher until it reached God. 'I'm here and I need you!' he screamed from his heart. 'Can't you see me?'

"A warmth covered John like a down comforter as he lay in that cot. He was by himself in that room of lost souls, but for the first time he could remember he allowed himself to not be alone. The siren song from the abyss was replaced with a spiritual melody that filled him with hope. The ache for the pleasure from the chemical high was replaced with the distaste for the pain of his lost identity. The pleasure of the flesh was replaced by a hunger of his soul. He became a man again.

"The next days, weeks, and months were not easy ones. On the plus side, he was able to look at himself in the mirror and not be repulsed, and knew that the love and devotion of his family had remained steadfast throughout his ordeal. The tough times; however, remained under his skin like a rash, the itches driving him crazy at times while the salve of his newfound faith began to heal him.

"I sat on that bench in the courtyard of this wonderful facility full of second chances feeling mesmerized and conflicted. Here was a man I admired for his skill in law and whom I trusted to give me sound advice. Yet here I was admiring him from a completely different angle. Not for what he knew, but for what he had survived. It was kind of like finding out that your doctor had been a prisoner of war.

"After the tour, we hugged and I promised to keep in touch. I drove home in silence as I replayed what just happened to me. I said a silent prayer for my friend and his family."

Izzy paused and rubbed his eye. It could have been a tear or an itch. I didn't ask. The imagery of the demons fighting over John filled my imagination, and I wondered what happened to him.

Chapter 8

Dirty Laundry

Izzy took a long drink of water to sooth his dry throat and continued. "Later that night as I was working on a painting in my studio, I began to feel a little 'off.' As I thought about John and his story I began to realize that my life experience over the past few years was not too far from his. I had also lost everything near and dear to me and I was at rock bottom. The specter of loneliness began to dig its talons into my heart. It began with a rumble in my stomach like I had eaten a too-old piece of pizza and a headache like you get when you've been in the sun too long. Unable to concentrate, I decided to do laundry. As I stuffed clothes in the washer I began to convulse. The tears began to flow uncontrollably and I started to shiver. I dropped to my knees and then on my side as I curled in a ball and began hitting the floor with my fist. My two dogs peered cautiously and curiously into the room. As I screamed they ran to the bedroom closet where they go when it thunders. 'Why is all this happening to me!' I screamed at God, who at that time looked an awful lot like a pile of dirty clothes.

"I would love to say that I had a burning bush experience then, but I have to say that if a pile of dirty clothes had begun to speak to me there's no way I would ever tell anyone! What DID happen was just as weird. It was not a voice, but it was as clear as a voice. It was a feeling. It said to me, 'It's going to be all right.' I screamed back at the feeling, 'Why did I lose everything?' It bounced right back at me, 'It's going to be all right.' As I laid on the floor in a blubbering mess with my nose running and spittle dripping down my chin, I weakly argued, 'What did I do to deserve this?' I got the calm reply 'It's going to be all right.' I had had enough. I wobbled to my feet and screamed at the hot water heater, 'But it's not all right!!' I swear I could sense the feeling inside me smile as it countered: 'I didn't say it IS all right. I said it's going TO BE all right.'

"As I stood there amidst my dirty clothes I realized my head didn't feel like it was caught in an elevator door anymore. My stomach was grumbling and I realized I was hungry for the first time that day. Hope had been fertilized in my heart. Was God speaking to me? Was it my imagination or was it just my dirty clothes? Knowing that I needed all the help I could get, I washed my clothes and thanked God. The seed of healing in my heart began to grow.

"As the weeks and months of my own rebuilding passed, I thought of John often and wondered why God put him back in the path of my life. I thought of all the sharefish in his story like the staff at Healing Home, especially the director. I kept my promise to him. I would call him about once every three months or so and would leave him a message if I got his voice mail letting him know that I was thinking about and praying for him. Sometimes he would call back and we would talk for a while. Sometimes I would just write him a little note. The last time we got together for lunch, he gave me a huge hug and told me how much it has meant to him for me to stay in touch with him. He has stayed clean. He has opened up his own law office and is doing very well. He is closer to his wife and his children than he has been in a long, long time. Most importantly, he is now close to God.

"I realized that in the small act of a phone call or a note to a friend I had become involved in something that was bigger than me. While reaching out my hand to him I was also pulling myself closer to God and forward into a new and healthy life. The life of a sharefish."

As Izzy finished his story, his phrase "the life of a sharefish" lingered in my head.

"Wow! What an amazing experience." I said. "He was a lucky guy. You did a good thing by reaching out to him. I had a friend who wasn't so lucky. Maybe I should have been more of a friend – a sharefish - to him."

"Interesting that you say that," Izzy replied. "I started thinking about people I had known throughout my life that had been sharefish to me. My family had always been incredible and my sisters and parents were awesome examples of being sharefish. I had friends who always seemed to show up or call or send a note at just the right time to lift my spirits a little. I also thought of people to whom I could have and maybe should have been more of a sharefish." Izzy's eyes began to sparkle again. He grinned as he said "I realized after a dozen or so 'should's' that I needed to quit 'shoulding' all over myself and concentrate on doing better from that point forward!"

Chapter 9

The Golden Rule

Izzy continued. "After my experience with my friend John, the Bible became different to me. I could relate much better to some of the stories I read in the Old Testament (especially Job!) and began to realize what God really wanted from me. Now listen to me very carefully here. This is what I felt he wanted from *me*. I get weary from all these TV preachers telling me that they know better than I do what God wants me to do. God speaks to different people in different ways. The truth of the matter is that nobody really *knows* what God is totally like. Even the Bible comes at God from a few different angles. Anyway, what I *do* know about God is that He is all about relationships and with me, what was broken with Him was my *relationship* with Him. It wasn't about a bunch of rules or battles between tribes. It was about something bigger than that. Don't just take my word for it. Look at just about any major religion in the world. You will find some version of what has been called the Golden Rule. You know what the Golden Rule is, don't you, Nyles?"

"Sure," I said confidently. "It means we need to treat people like we like to be treated."

"Right." Izzy continued. "In the book of Matthew in the Bible, it's written 'In everything, therefore, treat people the same way you want them to treat you, for this is the Law and the Prophets.' And in Luke it says 'Treat others the same way you want them to treat you.' In the part of the Bible the Jews read, or the Old Testament, it says in Leviticus, 'You shall not take vengeance, nor bear any grudge against the sons of your people, but you shall love your neighbor as yourself; I am the LORD.'"

Ordinarily, someone quoting the Bible sent shivers down my spine. Before I could get uncomfortable, Izzy startled me by reaching into a pocket on the dashboard and handing me a well-worn sheet of paper that was folded several times and had yellowed with age. On it was a list of religions from all over the world and their versions of the Golden Rule. As I scanned the list there were some religions I was familiar with and some religions I had never heard of before.

In Baha'ism: "If thou lookest toward justice, choose then for others what thou choosest for thyself. Blessed is he who prefers his brother before himself."

In Brahmanism: "This is the sum of duty: Do naught unto others which would cause you pain if done to you."

In Buddhism: "Hurt not others with that which pains yourself."

In Confucianism: "Is there one word which may serve as a rule to practice for all one's life? The Master said, 'Is not reciprocity (sympathy, consideration) such a word? What you do not want done to yourself, do not unto others.'"

In Hinduism: "The life-giving breaths of other creatures are as dear to them as the breaths of one's own self. Men gifted with intelligence and purified souls should always treat others as they themselves wish to be treated."

In Jainism: "Indifferent to worldly objects, a man should wander about, treating all creatures in the world as he himself would be treated."

In Islam: "No one of you is a believer until he loves for his brother what he loves for himself."

In Sikhism: "As thou deemest thyself, so deem others; then shalt thou become a partner in Heaven."

In Shintoism: "Irrespective of their nationality, language, manners and culture, men should give mutual aid, and enjoy reciprocal, peaceful pleasure by showing in their conduct that they are brethren."

In Taoism: "Regard your neighbor's gain as your own gain, and regard your neighbor's loss as your own loss."

In Zoroastrianism: "That nature alone is good which refrains from doing unto another whatsoever is not good for itself."

I stopped scanning the list and looked up at Izzy. "I've never even heard of some of these religions," I said. "Why are there so many if their main points are the same?"

"I'll tell you what I think, Nyles. It's a people thing, not a religion thing. God is so much bigger than we can ever imagine that we as humans sometimes can't stand it; so we try to make him fit into our little comfortable compartments. I'm a Christian and am very comfortable with my beliefs. What I have learned about Jesus makes me believe the way I do. I also believe that everyone has a story about why they believe what they do. I love to hear their stories and as you can tell, I love to tell mine and hope that people can find the happiness I now feel. As good as that feeling is, and even though the Bible says God made me in His image, what He was telling me in the Old Testament stories of pain and suffering was that no matter how good life may be, I would always falter and begin to put things ahead of my relationship with Him. Some people would call it "worshipping" those things since they would control my thoughts and actions. For me, those things were wealth and status. For you, it may be different. It became clear that neither wealth nor status is bad. They only become bad when they get in the way of Him.

"The great author C.S. Lewis says it best in his book <u>Mere Christianity</u> when he calls Pride the greatest sin. Pride is the hero of the selfish, but is irrelevant to the sharefish. You will notice that the sharefish do not spend energy trying to convince you to be like them. They want to help you become who God made *you* to be. As I explored the New Testament, this fundamental principle jumped off of the pages. When Jesus himself was asked what the greatest commandment was, do you remember what he said?

"Ummm…not really," I admitted, looking down.

"Don't worry about that, Nyles. In a minute you WILL know." Izzy grinned. "It's a great story. Jesus was surrounded by lots of people. The religious leaders of his day were trying to trick him into saying something so they could have him arrested or at least make him look foolish in front of the crowd of people. Finally, one of the religious leaders asked Jesus what the most important commandment was. Now, it doesn't say this anywhere, but I think he asked Jesus that because no matter what Jesus said, he would have to be saying that nine of the ten were less important and then they would have him where they wanted him.

"You notice the question wasn't about IF one was more important. It was about WHICH ONE was most important. Tricky folks, those religious leaders. There are some of those same religious folks around today you have to watch out for! Anyway, remember the Golden Rule? How about the Golden Rule super charged! Jesus calmly said to this religious leader and to the rest of the crowd that the most important commandment was to Love. Period. Number One, loving God with everything we have. And Number Two, loving each other as much as we love ourselves. The religious leader was hit right in the heart with those words. He had grown up in a culture where worshipping God was the center of his daily life. But loving God, loving each other, loving ourselves?

"He acknowledged in front of Jesus and the crowd that Jesus was right. It's not written anywhere, but I know the religious leader's buddies didn't like that at all! Jesus just looked at him, and I'm sure Jesus smiled as he told him how close to heaven the religious leader was. I've always wondered what happened to that religious leader. He had an unbelievable decision to make. One that would change his life forever. He had come from generations of "selfish" - people who felt that God was only accessible to a few privileged people under certain circumstances. Here comes this man, Jesus, who turned his world upside down by offering a life of being a "sharefish" through God. A God who loves everyone and who commands us to love everyone as well as ourselves. WOW! I pray that man made the right decision."

Chapter 10

Honor and Shame

"Wait a minute, Izzy," I interrupted. "My years of Bible school as a kid are coming back to me now. Of course God is for all people. Everybody knows that."

"Not so fast, my young friend," Izzy replied. "Back in that culture it was taught by the religious leaders that religion was very exclusionary. God was only in the temple. Only certain people were allowed in the temple. Most regular folks, even the minority who could read, were not allowed access to scripture. The few scrolls that were even in existence were tightly guarded and only read by priests and teachers. The thought of God loving everyone the same was preposterous and blasphemy. The religious leader's powerful position was at risk. He had a gut wrenching decision to make that not only affected his life – it affected his family's life as well. In that culture, a family's honor or shame was more sacred than the legal system."

"I didn't know that," I said. "So all these people who began to follow what Jesus taught them actually were going against their culture?"

Izzy paused for a minute. "Well, I'm no historian, but from what I've been able to find out you are probably very close to being right on the money. When the early followers of Jesus made their decision to become believers, they left most of their old lives behind. That was the point of Jesus being born. His birth was a miracle both in the Immaculate Conception, *and* in that he was born into this world as a baby like everyone else instead of appearing in a chariot from the sky as a man, a warrior or king, like everyone expected. That's why some people still don't believe he was and is the Son of God.

"The Jews were expecting a great warrior to come and rescue them from the tyranny of the Roman Empire. That's why they kept referring to the 'son of David' who would come and redeem them. When this carpenter's son grew up in a small village and in his early thirties began preaching that God was for everyone, not just a chosen race or class of people, it went against what everyone wanted their savior to be. That's another reason why some people don't believe he was and is the Son of God.

What the people failed to realize and continue to miss today, is that his death was an inconceivable act of grace for everyone. When Jesus was crucified on that cross, I believe all the stuff that makes people unworthy of the full love of God, died with him."

"Whoa, Izzy." I interrupted. "This stuff is where it all gets really confusing and quite frankly, kind of puts me off the way I've heard some people preach it. I'm starting to get your sharefish stuff and actually kind of like that idea. What I'm not getting is this Jesus stuff. If Jesus is the only way, then why is that list of 'isms' so long?"

Izzy took a deep breath. "I know it can be confusing, Nyles. Even the Christians can't agree on things! Some scholars list at least 22 major religions in the world, with thousands of subgroups. Christianity is one of those major religions. The term Christianity indicates the belief that Jesus Christ was the Son of God so you would think there would be some common ground. I had a hard time believing this, but there are at least 38,000 different denominations of Christians with each denomination taking a different stand on this whole Jesus thing. Of course, each of them thinks they have things exactly right. It's no wonder people are confused."

Izzy paused to let all this sink in. He finally said, "I'm sorry, Nyles. I feel a little like I'm preaching. You want me to stop?"

"Not now!" I replied. "I want you to list all 38,000 denominations!" We both laughed. "Seriously, Izzy, keep going. I've never heard some of this stuff before. Just know that I'm going to do my own research on this."

Izzy smiled. "Fair enough. You promise to let me know when you've had enough?"

"Yes, I promise. Please go on!" I said, my head beginning to swim with all this new information. I wanted more.

Izzy chuckled, which made me turn to him in surprise. He said through another chuckle. "I think God gets a pretty good laugh watching us."

"How so?" I asked, finding myself catching Izzy's contagious smile.

"Here we have all these religions with a common basis of being good to each other in the name of God, right? Yet we can't agree on how to go about it, which is why there are all these religions. On top of it all, even within the religions we can't agree, so we have to have multiple denominations or divisions within each of these divisions. We have disagreed for so long and have been so stubborn about it all that not only can we not come to the common conclusion that we need to actually act out what we believe by being good and respectful of each other, we hold the torch of our beliefs high as we go to war with each other to prove who is right."

Izzy had stopped smiling. He said softly, "The saddest part of it all is that there have been millions and millions of people killed because of this. In fact, an overwhelming majority of non-disease related deaths in our human history could be traced to this very disagreement. That part I don't think God likes very much."

I nodded at Izzy. "That's why a lot of us have given up on God," I admitted. "Not only do we not feel him in our lives, but we look at how religion has messed up our world and we wonder what the point of it all is."

Izzy was quiet for so long I went from looking out my window at yet another nameless town on the highway, wondering where in the world we were, to looking at him wondering what he was thinking. "You OK?" I offered.

After a time, he said softly, "It doesn't have to be that way."

My eyes caught Izzy's. I asked him a question to which I already knew the answer. "Is that where the sharefish come in?"

Izzy smiled gently, nodded slightly, and kept looking straight ahead.

I expected Izzy to tell me more about the sharefish. Instead, after a long pause, Izzy asked me, "Do you think you understand now how the culture was back in Jesus' day?"

I nodded, then realized that Izzy was looking straight ahead so I answered, "I think so. The religious people of that time were looking for a military man to come and rescue them from the Romans. Right?"

"Right," Izzy replied. "There had been centuries of wars between the tribes in that region. The Old Testament is full of stories about them. Each time the Israelites, or 'chosen people' as God called them in the Bible, would fall away from God, an angel would appear to someone and help them defeat their enemies. Sometimes that person would be just a common person, but with God on their side they were able to persevere and do some miraculous things and win the battle."

I interrupted. "But if God is a loving God, as you say he is, how could he cause all this war? If he can do anything, why didn't he just make people nicer so everyone could get along?"

"Great question," Izzy said. "There's been speculation, debate, and downright bloodshed itself on that very question. Here's what I think. I think it boils down to two things. Free will, and for lack of a better term, the antithesis to God. Let me explain. One of the side effects of the whole Adam and Eve thing with the Tree of Knowledge was that our free will became much more prominent to us. That means our ability to examine a situation and decide how we will respond to it became convoluted because our human side became much more tempting. We stopped thinking in a godly way and started thinking more selfishly, or 'stinkin' thinkin', as My mother used to call it."

"Before that, it's my belief that Adam and Eve's relationship with God was so powerful and good there was no need for contemplation. Adam and Eve had free will, and that will was freely and irresistibly drawn toward God. Each decision was obvious and there was no debate. To Adam and Eve, there was nothing but good in the world so all decisions were directed toward good. Satan tempted Adam and Eve with the opportunity to have their eyes opened like God's with the ability to see good and evil, and was somehow able to give them a taste of that power through the choice of whether to eat the fruit from the forbidden tree or not. They had the free will to choose. Beginning with the 'apple incident,' Adam and Eve's relationship with God began to deteriorate because the other side, the ungodly side, was brought more prominently into their decision making and consequently into ours today. Sometimes we make the right choices. Sometimes we don't. The bottom line is our expanded free will resulted in us falling away from our closeness with God.   Personally, I think this is a great illustration of the sharefish principle and God.

"Think about it, Nyles. When we pray to God, how do we normally begin our prayers?"

"At the risk of this being a trick question, I'll say 'Our Father'?" I quipped.

"Correct! Give the man bonus points." Izzy smiled. "So, here's yet another example of how we as humans think we know more about God than we really do. Did you know there are almost twenty different names for God just in the Old Testament, with some of them actually being plural?"

"Wait just a minute!" I interrupted. "Are you trying to tell me that there is more than one God?" The shivers began up my spine again and I was torn between telling him to let me out of the truck right there and listening to his answer.

"Not at all, Nyles," he said softly but with purpose. "What I'm telling you is that God is way more than we as human beings can even describe. While this can be a great and wonderful thing, it makes it very difficult for us to accept. With all the names he was called in the Old Testament, it makes it much more comfortable for us to pray to him as Our Father instead of any of the 17 or so different names he is referred to in the Old Testament. Why? The two most common names God is called in the Old Testament, which was originally written in Hebrew, are Elohim, which means God as Creator and Preserver, and Yawheh, which means "I am."

In that culture the closest thing in the daily lives of the people they could relate that to was the head of each household, which was the father. The father was considered the creator of the offspring which was an extremely important point of honor. A man's standing in the community as well as self-esteem was dependent upon his ability to sire many children, especially male children. God became Father God, God the Father, even though he was and still is so much bigger than any description. People needed to have some kind of relational point from which to pray and worship."

Chapter 11

Too Big For Words

"**R**emember, Nyles, as I said before, this is just what *I* believe. If you choose to travel the road of spiritual discovery, you may come up with your own explanations. I would be a hypocrite to tell you not to let people tell you how to believe and then tell you that you must believe what and how I believe! My calling is to share with you what I believe, and to be an example of that belief by caring about you," Izzy said with sincerity.

"Here's where the sharefish come in. No matter what else they believe, the common thread to almost all of them is that people are to take care of each other. That's because sharefish believe that God wants to take care of us and God wants us to be like Him. When I say 'like Him' it illustrates another example of how we narrow the magnificent scope of God. This time into a gender. Since we don't have a word in our vocabulary to truly describe the magnificence of God, we have to just say God. Since we don't have a non-gender word to describe God, we just default to 'Him.' He may be called Creator, Provider, Healer, Righteousness, Shepherd or, even just 'I am.'

"The bottom line is this, God is indescribably awesome!! God couldn't be described then and He still can't be. The closest thing to a description is the word "Love." The good news for us is, this indescribably awesome God loves each of us in a unique and wonderful way and wants a personal relationship with each and every one of us. That's what the selfish religious culture of Jesus' time couldn't get their arms around. By saying they were trying to keep God holy, the religious leaders became very powerful and influential by filtering God to the people and filtering the people to God.

"And that, my friend Nyles, was why God sent his son Jesus to that place and time, and ultimately why he died. He was the holy sharefish sent to a selfish world.

"God has always wanted us to get back to the relationship with Him that he originally had with Adam and Eve. I call it 'getting right with God.' The big difference now is, we have to decide that's what *we* want as well. We have free will to choose this path or not. For Christians, Jesus is there to fill in the gap that makes that possible again. It made an almost impossible thing as easy as a decision. The religious leaders of that time were afraid of God being that easy for people to have a relationship with, so they had to do something to stop it."

"Boy, I'm glad it's not that way now," I said.

Izzy startled me with his laugh. "It's *exactly* the same now, Nyles. Once you find your path with God and decide to take it, you leave your old ways behind and begin to see things in a completely new way. Of course, we are human and tend to be oblivious to God working in our lives sometimes, just like those religious leaders back in Jesus' culture. At least *I* am sometimes." Izzy laughed again. "It reminds me of a time when I didn't make it too easy for God to introduce me to another sharefish and to be one myself. Care to hear about it?"

I realized I genuinely liked this man. No pretense. No holier-than-thou stuff. Just a good person. I laughed to myself as I mentally described him as…well, a sharefish. I also felt he was sincere when he told me he would stop whenever I had had enough. I was not there yet.

I wanted to make sure Izzy knew that I was interested in hearing his story. I turned to him and grinned. "Sure. Go ahead. I'm all ears."

Chapter 12

Delta Blues

"**A** group of us from our church went on a week long
mission trip to the Mississippi Delta in Johnsonville, Arkansas. It is
in one of the 10 poorest counties in the country. The number one
source of income in the area is welfare, followed closely by drugs.
We had sports camps, Bible school, and other events for the kids.
We were given necklaces with wooden crosses on them to give to
someone in whom we felt God's love working. Tuesday night was
game night at the Activity Center, which is an old Armory hanger
slowly being renovated. I was tired and did not want to go. I had
been playing baseball with the kids in 100-degree heat all day and
my back hurt. I thought about just staying in my room at the
church where we were staying and getting some rest. 'It will be
chaos there,' I told myself. 'I really need to stay here and recharge.'
Some of the group wanted to go and needed someone to drive

them. I finally compromised with my conscience and decided that I would go and just stay for a little while.

"I was walking around meeting some of the local people who had come to the event. It was a madhouse. There were kids playing, people running, music was blaring from the loud speakers, laughter and squeals erupted from the various games that were taking place, and the constant buzz of dozens of conversations filled in any gaps in the chaos. Several hundred people were enjoying themselves and the event. I noticed two men toward the end of one of the bleachers. Even though the place was packed, they seemed to have been carved out and isolated by the crowd. No laughter. No conversation. Just the two of them. I walked over and introduced myself.

" 'Good evening, sir,' he said. 'My name is Sammy Blues Jones.' With this area being known as one of the birthplaces of blues music, the name seemed appropriate. His face was the face of a man who had seen a lot of heartache in his life, his eyes drawn down on the outside corners as if weighed down by the crow's feet wrinkles that emanated from them. His old flannel shirt was too small, the sleeves just coming down to two inches above his wrist bone. He looked to be in his late fifties or early sixties but in this part of the country the heat, the work, and the poverty tended to age people quickly so I couldn't be sure.

"He surprised me when he said, 'This is my son, Michael. Michael Jones. He can't speak.'

"I had noticed that even though there was a great deal of energy in the community center, the son had been staring blankly at the wall across the room all evening. 'How old is Michael?' I asked Mr. Jones. 'Thirty years old,' he said. Wow. He looked no older than 18. His hair was cropped short and he wore a clean blue shirt that was buttoned all the way up even though it had to be 90 degrees in the gym. 'Nice to meet you both,' I said and moved on to another conversation with a group of kids that I had played baseball with earlier that afternoon. After about 15 minutes I felt drawn back to Mr. Jones and Michael.

"I looked Mr. Jones in the eyes and told him something that I have felt all my life: 'Mr. Jones, I want you to know that I have always believed that people like your son are closer to God than we will ever be because they are not tainted by worldly things like we are.' His eyes glistened as he replied, 'God bless you, sir.'

"Having done my time that I had promised my conscience, I drove our group back to the church so I could finally get some rest. I could not get comfortable. Something deep in my soul was stirring about my encounter with Mr. Jones and his son. I could not get them off of my mind. 'Go back' something told me. Why, I wondered. What else could I say? I fought the feeling with all my might. Thirty minutes later I reached up and touched the cross that was still hanging around my neck.

"I rushed back to the community center. 'Please still be there,' I prayed. I searched through the crowd. There they were, still by themselves. 'I had to come back,' I told Mr. Jones, 'There's something I need to ask you.' He gave me the puzzled look of someone who had been told what to do for most of his life and had rarely been *asked* anything. I breathed deep and continued. 'Mr. Jones, we were given these crosses to remind us about God's love. We are supposed to give ours to someone special as an act of faith. What I need to ask is… May I give mine to Michael?' Mr. Jones smiled approvingly, his eyes lighting up and the crow's feet wrinkles deepening and pointing upward. I moved over in front of Michael. As I took the necklace from around my neck I was astounded to see Michael bow his head. As I put the necklace around his neck I told Michael that God loved him. He raised his head. On his face was the most serene smile I have ever seen. I looked at his father. As tears streamed down his worn face, he smiled and grabbed my hand. 'You have made him very happy. Thank you.'

" 'I know what you mean, Mr. Jones,' I said. 'God is awesome. To Him be the glory.'

"As I walked back to the car I realized that I wasn't so tired any more. I wept openly as I drove back to the church. I realized that it wasn't about me giving my cross to what the world would consider a poor, lonely, disabled, marginalized man. God wanted to revive my spirit through His wonderful creation, Michael, and his angelic father, Sammy Blue. They may be marginalized on earth, but I believe that in God's kingdom they are held tightly. They both are wonderful examples of Paul's letter to the Thessalonians in the Bible where he expresses courage and tender care, and how important it is to lead a life worthy of God.

"God has a wonderful way of taking something we fight, something we discard, something we think of as useless, be it an event, or time, or people, and making them beacons in our path that lead us to our Creator. In my heart, when I think of examples of what I should strive to be in my faith, I will always think of my brothers in Christ, Sammy Blue and Michael Jones. My experience with them was bigger than me.

"Another sharefish moment."

Chapter 13

An Opposing Force

"See, Nyles? There it was right in front of me and I couldn't see it."

I sighed. "That's an awesome story, Izzy. Why hasn't anything like that ever happened to me?"

It was Izzy's turn to sigh and shake his head. "Funny thing about the Bible," he finally said with a grin. "The more you read it, the more sharefish opportunities just seem to happen. This does not happen without an element of danger, however."

"What?" I asked. "Did you say it could be dangerous to read the Bible?"

Izzy took a deep breath, and the furrow between his eyebrows deepened. "Remember when I told you there were two things in the way of our relationship with God, with our free will being the first? Well the second thing is powerful and messes with our free will. People call it different things: Satan, dark side, whatever. Now, I believe there is only one God and that is God. This "other side" is no deity, but according to the Bible it wanted to be. Since it can't be what it wants to be it does the next best thing. Put whatever name on it you want to, but its main purpose is to keep you from pursuing a relationship with God.

"Sometimes I think it's indescribable too since it has so many forms and is so sneaky. That's why you'll see people focused on a part of their religion that is not about taking care of each other. As humans, we are very susceptible to earthly things. We'll offer great blessings if you will send us your money. We'll justify horrible actions by taking a verse out of context. We'll discriminate against a particular group of people because they are 'unworthy.' We will persecute people because they do not believe what we believe. We will spend a great deal of time pointing out what others are doing 'wrong' if you haven't fallen lock-step into our belief system.

"Don't misunderstand me. People very often are good hearted and are trying to fulfill their vision of 'good religion.' People will even defiantly justify their position as being 'called by

God.' You can tell it is not of God because these actions are selfish actions. In fact, there is much finger pointing about 'being sinful.' You know what sin is, Nyles? Sin is whenever you do something that is hurtful – to your spiritual growth, to someone else, or to God. I call this side the Side of Dis-grace because it is the opposite of God's love and His intention for us to lead a life of grace like Him.

"I believe God wants us to be sharefish. Instead of wanting your money for their own personal gain, sharefish will ask you to help them help other people. Instead of harming other people, they will put themselves in harm's way to help those in need. Sharefish will not value people according to some rules of 'worth' because they realize that we are all children of God.

Though I was caught up in the excitement of Izzy's story, I could not shake an uneasy question I wanted to ask. Finally, I blurted out 'What about all the wars – in the Bible and in the world's history? Won't the selfish just run over the sharefish?'

Izzy looked at me straight in the eyes and grinned from ear to ear. "Nope. I don't want to spoil it for you, but I've read the Bible all the way to the end. God wins." He laughed a hearty laugh.

"Don't make the mistake of thinking that being a sharefish is a wimpy thing. It's not about giving everything you have to anyone who asks or acquiescing to everyone else's desires. It's about doing the right thing and standing up for what you feel is right, even when it is not popular or profitable. When you are a sharefish you feel a significance that many people have tried and failed to find using earthly standards for success.

"You tell me, Nyles. Who do you think exhibits the following characteristics, a selfish or a sharefish? Courage, empathy, confidence, empowerment, compassion, strength, gratitude and resolve?"

I replied, "I think I'm getting it. It would take a sharefish to be courageous enough to do some of the things necessary to take care of others. You would have to empathize with people to be on their level. You would have to have incredible inner strength and confidence to combat what the world will say about you. I can also see how you would be immensely grateful for what you have and for the ability to help people who need help. "

Izzy nodded and smiled while scratching his chin. "Wow, you've come a long way since Oregon, my young friend. Before I get into the God and wars thing, which can be a pretty 'sticky wicket' as they say, may I share an experience that shows examples of the sharefish characteristics?"

"It's going to be tough to beat that last one," I challenged.

Chapter 14

A Dirt Road and a Rock in My Shoe

Izzy took a long drink of water. He thought for a while, painting the picture of his story in his mind. His eyes began to squint a little and he smiled softly, indicating to me that Izzy was reliving a wonderful memory. He cleared his throat, settled in his seat, and pressed the gas pedal to pass a car and began to ease into his story as he eased back into the right lane.

"I was in Honduras one time walking down the road in a small village there. It always amazes me how the smallest things, if we will allow ourselves to be aware of them, can change our lives and the people around us forever. In this case, it was a bell. The school bell. It startled me when it rang. Children raced out of the classroom to squeeze every precious moment of the one-hour recess.

"The school was a simple two classroom building in the small Honduran village of Rio de Bautismo on the river just outside of Choluteca. The faded green and red paint on the outside of the concrete building blended with the banana, cashew and mango trees. The structure was built by the German Red Cross after Hurricane Mitch devastated the area in 1998.

"The children in their uniforms played with old tires or frayed lengths of jump rope. The white shirts and navy blue pants of the boys and the white blouses and navy blue skirts of the girls contrasted with the poverty that surrounded them. Smoke curled from houses made of sticks and mud with dirt floors as the mothers of the house made and cooked fresh tortillas over open fires to sell at a local open air market.

"The bell rang to indicate the end of recess, beckoning the children back to their seats. Not all the children. Eight-year-old Maria sadly watched from the gate in front of the school as the children scurried back into the building to their desks.

"Maria's nickname in the village was Pelo, which means 'lots of hair,' because when she was a baby she had a head of wild thick hair. She still did.

"She captured my heart the moment I first saw her. Twenty of us from our church had come to this village in two teams to

102

work with members of the Rio de Bautismo congregation to help them build a much-needed sanctuary. They were currently using a small building not much bigger than a tool shed. We worked hard and we played hard in the 100-degree heat. Games of soccer and Frisbee would break out after school and there was always someone under a tree coloring with the crayons and coloring books we brought. Children from the village crowded around our mission team patiently… well almost patiently… as they took turns writing their names for us in the small notebooks we took just for that purpose. Not Maria.

"Maria hid behind our pick-up truck, peering around the fender, her sad brown eyes glistening with tears of estrangement. Her angelic face was dirty, her hair was a tangled mess, and her clothes were tattered. She looked like a child's doll that someone had left in the back yard and forgotten.

"I soon learned why she was so sad. It wasn't because of the poverty; everyone in this village had very little in the way of material things. But even in this marginalized village, her family was marginalized. She and her family lived in a small one-room shack on the outskirts of the village on the way to the river. I was never quite sure how many brothers and sisters she had. Her father worked in the sugar cane fields when he could and her mother made tortillas for the open-air market.

"Every dollar they made went to feeding the family. They could not afford a uniform and school supplies for Maria so she was not allowed to go to school. It was yet one more way she felt like a misfit.

"My heart broke. I prayed for guidance. There was so much need throughout the village, and we had been instructed not to do things directly for individuals, but only through the minister whose new cinder block sanctuary we were building. There was something about Maria that gave me an itch in my soul. My dear friend Ricardo calls it 'a rock in my shoe for God.' Through the dirt and tatters I saw great potential and I just could not shake it. Throughout the day I tried to think of other things, but thoughts of helping her in some way kept popping into my head.

"As the children gathered around the next day to sign our notebooks, I kept looking around for Maria. I finally saw her sitting under a tree in the courtyard across the street. '¡Buenos dias, Maria!' I said as I walked across the yard toward her. She had on the same tattered clothes she had on the day before. Startled, she quickly looked up at me and then back down to the scribbling she had been working on in the dirt at her feet. I knelt beside her and put my hand on her shoulder and she glanced back at me. I caught her beautiful brown eyes with mine and said sincerely, 'Dios te ama, Maria.' I wanted her to know that not only did God know who she was, He loved her as well.

"Her inquisitive look seemed to say that she had not been told very often that she was loved, much less by God. I became overwhelmed with emotion. I did not want her to misinterpret my tears so I stood back up, patted her on the head, told her again that God loved her, and walked away. I took the long way back to the construction site so I could compose myself.

"For the rest of the day, whenever I would see her I would smile at her and wink. In time she would give me a shy smile. By the middle of the week she would give me a quick smile and answer 'Bien' when I would ask her how she was doing with my poorly spoken Spanish, '¿Como esta, Maria?'

"Throughout the week I wrestled with how to help her get into school, which I felt would help her feel included in the village and give a boost to her self esteem. If I gave her family the money to pay for her uniform, shoes and school supplies I thought they might save the money and use it for food, and I could understand that.

"I prayed about it and on Thursday I got what I considered enough of a sign to take action. Some children had gathered to write their names in my notebook. Maria walked up to see what was going on. I handed her my pen and asked her to write her name in my notebook. She took my notebook and became very focused as she wrote. She smiled proudly as she handed it back. On the page were small circles with lines between them. 'Muy bien,' I told her as I simultaneously fought back tears while giving her a high five. She could not even write her own name.

"That did it. I walked with one of my best friends to Maria's house. We asked her mother and father for permission to go and get what Maria needed to start school. With a skeptical look, they agreed. We then went to the school to talk with the teacher about Maria and to help us compile a list of the school supplies she needed for the school year. The teacher was excited to help. She knew Maria and promised to take good care of her. I took a pen and made an outline of Maria's feet so I could get her some shoes. I was not going to let one more day go by with Maria on the outside of that school gate.

"We went to the store in downtown Choluteca and loaded up. We drove back to the village and pulled back up to the construction site. After working for a while, we waited for a break in the workflow to quietly leave the area and get the bags of goodies out of the vehicle. As we walked up the dirt road to Maria's mud and stick house, I felt a lump start to form in my throat. We called out '¡Hola!' to announce our arrival as we headed up the path to the house. Maria's beautiful brown eyes peered from around the scrap wood doorframe. My friend explained to her mother what we had done. She put her hands on the sides of her face in disbelief. Tears began to streak down her face as she hugged us both continually saying 'Gracias, gracias, muchas gracias.' It was an unimaginable moment.

"There was only one thing that could have made it better for me, and that one thing happened. As I handed Maria her new pink back pack full of supplies and put her new school shoes by her dusty feet, she gave her mother a puzzled look. Her mother nodded to her and told her that she was going to school on Monday. Her eyes widened and she smiled the biggest smile I have ever seen. She wrapped her little arms around my neck and squeezed. She then opened her bag and took each item out and studied it carefully, like a child opening gifts on Christmas morning.

"As we left I said a silent prayer, thanking God for giving me this opportunity to help Maria, one of His angels on earth. I'm not sure my feet touched the road the whole way back to the worksite.

"Two days later we celebrated the first Sunday service in the new sanctuary. It was standing room only. Pastor Carlitos stood behind the simple podium and we all sang songs of thanksgiving.

"I kept looking for Maria but did not see her. I wondered if she was okay and continued to turn and survey the crowd as we sang. We finished singing and Pastor Carlitos began to speak. I took one more look behind me and there she was, walking up the center aisle toward me in what was obviously her best dress, a plain pink one with white trim. It was clean and so was she. As if waiting for an invitation, she paused and looked at me with her angelic brown eyes. I waved for her to come and sit with me. She ran the last few steps and climbed in my lap. My heart leapt from my chest as I beamed. It seemed like I could understand Spanish as Pastor Carlitos gestured toward heaven in thanksgiving for the blessing of the new sanctuary. Blessings have no language barrier.

"The next morning we packed our gear and headed to the airport in Tegucigalpa. As we crossed the bridge leaving Choluteca, I looked down the river toward Rio de Bautismo and smiled.

"In my mind I could see Maria sitting on the front row in her new white blouse and navy blue skirt, her new shoes on her tiny little feet. She had her new pencil in her hand, and her tongue was sticking out of the corner of her mouth as she concentrated on her work. This time there were no circles with lines coming from them on her paper.

"She was writing her name."

Chapter 15

The List

"Wow." I said softly. "That must have been an incredible feeling. I could see the sharefish characteristics as you told your story. I understand now that the more you do for other people the more you get out of it as well."

I waited for Izzy to congratulate me for being so right. Instead he paused for what seemed like an eternity. Finally, he said slowly, "Okay, tell me who you think of that has led a life of a sharefish."

"Hmmmm…Let me see. Mother Teresa, Gandhi, Martin Luther King, Jr.,…am I on the right track?" I asked him.

"Fascinating!" Izzy's eyes danced and gleamed. "What strikes you about your list?" he asked me.

"Hmmmm... well, they all did great things for other people and it seems they all had the characteristics you talked about. Why are you grinning?"

Izzy could barely contain himself. "You are right on target, Nyles; however there are three things about your list that you should really take to heart.

"First, notice that they all had foundations in different religions and countries. A sharefish is not limited by geography or religion.

"Second, they helped people who were not necessarily like themselves. Their cause was bigger than demographics. When you are a sharefish, you realize that *all* are God's children. Even though I was excited when I saw her in church that Sunday, no one asked Maria what church she belonged to before we helped her. I have no idea whether Sammy Blue Jones and his son were Methodist, Jewish, or Muslim or what neighborhood they lived in or what Mr. Jones did for a living.

"Third, and this is very important, for every one person on any sharefish list you make up, there are literally millions of people you have never heard of that should also be on your list. People who make themselves aware each day of ways that they can positively affect someone else's life, and actually act on it. One of the really neat things about sharefish is that they don't need or even want publicity. They don't spend enough time thinking of themselves to care. People who lead a sharefish life do not think less of themselves, they just think of themselves *less*. They realize that getting closer to God is not a competition. God is big enough for everyone and knows each of us by name. Even the three wonderful human beings you named did not use publicity to elevate themselves. They used it to further their cause to help people."

"So what is the biggest sharefish thing you've ever done, Izzy?" I inquired.

Izzy quickly replied with a smile. "Like I just said, it's not a competition, Nyles." Izzy reached over and playfully punched Nyles in the arm. "I will tell you something I did that was incredibly cathartic and helped get me in the frame of mind I needed to be to become more of the sharefish I was meant to be. It was one of the most difficult and at the same time easiest things I have ever done and was emotionally very powerful for me."

"Sounds interesting." I urged. "Please go on."

Izzy cleared his throat. "I knew that to get where I needed to be with God there were some things that I needed to say to some folks. I made three lists. One list was everyone I felt had been a sharefish to me. The second list was everyone I felt I had hurt in some way in my past. And the third..."

"Yes?" I encouraged. "The third?"

"The third list had three names on it. People who had caused me the deepest pain. My ex-wife, the man she had the affair with, and her father."

"Now you really have me interested," I said. "What did you do with the lists?"

Izzy scratched his chin. "I cut all the names out and put them in a small box. Every week I would pull out a name. If they were on list one, I would call them or write them to thank them for being such a positive influence on me. I had some amazing conversations and in some cases renewed relationships that had been stale for over 20 years. If the name I drew came from list two, I did the same thing. I would call them or write them and apologize for hurting them." Izzy laughed. "I had some pretty interesting conversations with some of those folks too! You know, the weird thing was that most of them had no recollection of the event where I hurt them, but were appreciative just the same. Some even said they were going to make a list of their own."

"What about the list with the three names?" I asked, and immediately felt I had overstepped my bounds.

Izzy paused for a minute and sighed. "Yeah, whenever I would draw a name I would feel a ping of dread as I looked at it for fear it was one of those three. When the first of those names came up, I stared at if for a while hoping it would change before my eyes. It didn't. It was my ex-wife's name. It sat on the counter for a day or two while I decided how I wanted to contact her. Truth be told, I was stalling a bit. Like most things in life, though, the doing it wasn't as tough as the *thinking* about doing it." Izzy cut his eyes over in my direction. "Sometimes our imaginations are not our friends, Nyles. Anyway, I took a deep breath and called her. We had a remarkable conversation that helped us both put a lot behind us so we could both move on. She was contrite, yet understanding and sincerely happy for me. I'll always appreciate her for that. She had moved to Colorado, was engaged, and was pursuing a career as a veterinarian. For the first time I could remember, she seemed really happy. After we talked, I kicked myself for putting it off as long as I did. As soon as I hung up the phone I decided that I didn't want to dread picking a name wondering if it would be one of the other two, so I fished around in the box and took their names out. I put them on my counter and thought and prayed for a week. Then I got two blank greeting cards, you know the ones with a picture on the front with nothing on the inside? I addressed the envelopes with no return address and took each card and wrote one word on the inside. No salutation. No signature. In bold letters I wrote **FORGIVEN.** I put the cards in the mail. I don't know if they got the cards or not, but it doesn't matter. In my heart I have forgiven them. That is huge for me. God showed me a lot of good stuff in that little exercise."

I replied enthusiastically: "That's a pretty neat idea, Izzy. I…" I did a quick mental calculation of how long my "forgiving" list would be and quickly decided to change the subject. "OK, I'm getting the point about the good side of God, but…" I paused. "If God is so good, what about all those stories in the Bible where it talks about God telling people to kill people and go to war. That doesn't sound like a sharefish God to me." I felt both relieved and guilty. Relieved I had the courage to ask and guilty for changing the mood of the conversation.

Izzy must have recognized both feelings. He acknowledged my question with a nod and gave me a kind, reassuring smile.

"Thanks for reminding me, Nyles. The direct answer is that no one knows for sure. I'm not trying to dodge the issue. It's an important one. I've done my share of exploring this one myself and still have more questions than answers. I do have a possible explanation that I'll share with you.

"Keep in mind that these battles in the Bible had been handed down in oral tradition for thousands of years. It was common practice for victors in battle to exclaim that God was with them in victory. Please understand what I'm saying here. There are lifelong biblical scholars who will swear on their family name that the Bible is exactly accurate word for word. There are also lifelong biblical scholars who will tell you that when these stories were finally written down, there may have been some literary license used.

"For instance, if you study the life of Abraham you will find almost two dozen different accounts about his life, which is fascinating when you consider that he is a central figure for the Jews, Christians, and Muslims. The Hebrew word for it is "midrash" and it does not in any way change the holiness of the Bible. It is what it is. I'll leave it up to you to follow your heart on it. I have to admit I find it interesting that even people who have dedicated their lives to studying the Bible from a technical standpoint can't agree on exactly what it says.

"Here's another point about God and war to consider. Throughout the ages, leaders have said that God told them to lead their people against another, less godly, foe. Look them up sometime, you'll see. Need some examples? Here are some of the more infamous ones of how people did things because "God told me to." God told Constantine in the fourth century to make Christianity the Roman state religion. God told the seventh and eighth century Muslims to drive Christians and Jews from the Holy Land and to drive Christians from North Africa. God told the Catholic church of Spain to institute the Inquisition. God told Christians of England to expel the Jews in the 12th century. God told Joan of Arc to reclaim her homeland in the 15th century. God told the Russian Orthodox Church to persecute the Jews in what came to be known as the pogroms in the 19th century. God told Hitler and his followers in Lutheran and Catholic Europe to finish solving the 'Jewish problem,' as they called it. There are hundreds of stories like this.

"Nyles, I wasn't in the room when God spoke to any of these people so I can't tell you what's true and what's not. I *can* say that you have to be very, very careful when you are trying to listen to God because sometimes the dark side is very crafty and can sound an awful lot like him. Putting it to the sharefish test is a great help when this happens. Does this make sense, Nyles?" He turned to see if he had put me to sleep. "Nyles?"

Chapter 16

A New Look at an Old Psalm

I was so overwhelmed I could not speak. I had heard about
all these events throughout history but had not heard about the
God connection. Not that I doubted Izzy, but I made a mental
note to learn more about this. "I'm OK." I said. "My head is
spinning a little with all this stuff. I knew these people in history
had done some bad things, but I didn't know that they had said
God wanted them to do them. That's why I've been so skeptical
about all this. I remember reading in the Bible about all the rules
and violence and it didn't seem like God was very nice. So if
people are still doing all this bad stuff in God's name, what about
Jesus?"

"Nyles, the list is very long there. Some folks say that the
main reason Jesus came to earth in the first place was to experience

what being human was like so he could explain it to his Father. And he did. When he was on the cross he asked his Father to forgive us all. Why? Because we don't know what we are doing. It wasn't because Jesus didn't try to teach us. Even when he was on the cross he was still teaching us. A selfish will tell you that faith is no good because even Jesus lost his faith when he was on the cross because he cried out "My God, my God, why has thou forsaken me?" A sharefish, on the other hand, will point you to Psalm 22. Not the 23rd Psalm. The one before it. Have you ever read Psalm 22, Nyles?"

"I don't think so," I admitted.

"Guess how it starts," Izzy grinned.

"Um… something about a shepherd?" I lamely suggested.

"Nope. Don't be disappointed. Most folks don't. I find it fascinating that right beside the best-known scripture passage in the Bible is one that in my opinion is just as powerful but hardly anyone knows it. Psalm 22 begins with 'My God, my God, why have you forsaken me?'

"You're kidding," I gasped.

Izzy reached in the console in between the two seats and pulled out a weathered old Bible and handed it to me. "Psalms is in the middle," Izzy winked. Even though I hadn't held a Bible in my hands for over 15 years it felt weirdly comfortable. I impressed myself by how quickly I found Psalms and flipped the worn pages until I found Psalm 22. Sure enough, there it was. "My God, my God, why have you forsaken me?" I read softly.

Izzy startled me by saying, "Isn't that amazing? Here Jesus was going through the unspeakable torture of being crucified and he was still trying to give the good news of God's love to the people around him! If you read the rest of the chapter, you will be amazed at how it chronicles what Jesus experienced in his life including verse 18 where it says, "They divide my garments among them, and for my clothing they cast lots." Did you know that the Roman soldiers cast lots, kind of like dice, for Jesus' clothes that day? Did you know this Psalm was composed almost a thousand years earlier? Oh yes, my friend, Jesus did some incredible things for us. While on earth, he walked his talk. He was the ultimate sharefish. When he died, he asked his Father to forgive us for not being what He wants us to be. He was God's child. He could have asked for anything. Instead, he offered us everything."

Izzy scratched his chin. "If people would be sharefish like God wants us to, then that would take care of just about every polarizing subject out there. War, abortion, crime, abject poverty, ethnic cleansing, apartheid, you name it. Remember what I told you Jesus instructed the religious leaders about the most important commandment?

I quickly replied, "Yes. Love God with everything you've got and love your neighbor and love yourself."

"Right." Izzy said. "Almost 90 percent of the world's population who are asked say that they believe in God. Name one abomination this world is facing that would still exist if we all did what Jesus said to do, or for that matter what each of the major religions say to do, like we talked about before."

"Wow." I gasped. "I see your point. Boy, God must really be disappointed with us."

"Maybe. No one knows for sure. One thing I do know. If you believe what the Bible says then you know that God loves us anyway. Just like a good earthly father unconditionally loves his children, God's wonderful light of grace is unconditional just like His love. I fail at being what God wants me to be every day, because I'm human and because the dark side is crafty and knows my weak spots. Whenever I fall, I get back up on my knees, ask God to please forgive me and to give me the strength to learn from my failure and to do better next time.

Since God loves me like His own child, God loves me anyway, in spite of my shortcomings. When I accept that love, I begin to have the relationship with God that He has always wanted with me. I become a sharefish of God. There is nothing more beautiful. There is nothing more energizing. There is nothing more miraculous. There is nothing more powerful. There is nothing more dependable."

"All this sounds great," I said. "But it can't really be as simple as this, can it?"

Izzy continued, the furrow in his brow deepened once more. "It's the simplest yet most complex thing in the world. It's kind of like trying to explain water to someone who has never seen and experienced it. Try as you may, you can only get so much across to them of its beauty, of its versatility, of its necessity, of its power. Then suppose you are able to show them pictures of a bottle of water, a cloud, some snow, perhaps a lake, a river, and a stream. As they look at each of these pictures and you tell them stories about the images in the picture and how they are related to one another, they understand water much better and perhaps want to experience water themselves. This is like reading the Bible and each of these pictures are the books of the Bible. As you read and discover and experience God through the characters and stories of the Bible, you come much closer to fully understanding how magnificent God is."

The blue grass of Kentucky gleamed in the sunshine like someone had put shag carpeting over the softly undulating hills. Everything seemed livelier, clearer. The horses seemed to smile at me as they galloped within their white fences. Like looking through the lens of a camera, things I had experienced in my life were becoming more focused. Connections between my heart and my head were being made for the first time in my life. I still had far more questions than I had answers, and I felt totally comfortable with that.

Chapter 17

Immersion

Izzy's spiritual energy was contagious as he continued with his illustration.

"It starts getting really good now," Izzy grinned. "Once someone begins to learn about this marvelous water and how good it is, he wants to learn more and become more aware of it. Of course in our example the water is a metaphor for spirituality. Once someone has the seed of 'water' planted, he begins to see people differently. This new 'student of water' notices that everyone is carrying some form of water with them that looks like the pictures they saw. Some people are carrying small jars of water and only talk with people who have jars exactly like theirs.

"Other people may be dripping wet yet don't realize it and ignore everyone around them. Still others walk through puddles, shake their feet, and keep going. There are hosts of others who have a certain glow about them and are walking around with large pitchers of water and stop often and pour glasses of water for people as they interact with them. Others seem to exude a fine mist that engulfs and refreshes everyone they come in contact with. These people have an amazing peace about them.

"The student continues walking and for some reason is led down a path over a hill. Suddenly, as he looks up, his breath is taken away. He sees the most incredible body of water he has ever seen, a place where all the clouds and streams and rivers eventually end up. He feels something inside that can't be explained. The cool breeze blowing through his hair beckons him to the body of water. He thinks he should be afraid, but notices that the closer he gets the more comfortable he feels... like he is coming home...the way home is supposed to feel.

"As he reaches down and dips his hands in the water and feels its cool velvety fingers drip down his arms, he realizes that he has found the thing, the one thing, that he has felt emptiness for his entire life. Any guilt he may feel for not being the person he knows he should be evaporates like smoke in the wind. Even though he knows that he didn't do anything to deserve this feeling, he senses that this was meant exactly for him. He can almost hear the great water laugh joyously as he immerses himself in it, feeling truly alive for the first time. He fully understands the stories he heard. He can now comprehend the pictures he saw. He drinks and splashes and swims and dives and sings and feels whole. When he steps out of the water, he realizes that he is carrying that same feeling with him and knows that it will always be with him no matter where he goes."

Izzy pulled the truck over into the parking lot of another diner, turned and looked straight into my eyes.

"THAT'S what experiencing the Love and Grace of God is like."

Izzy's eyes had moistened. "Then, imagine if you suddenly began to wonder why all those people on the other side of the hill were keeping their little bits of water in a tightly sealed jar while others were sharing their water with everyone they met. Why do you think they would do that, Nyles?"

I thought for a moment. "I guess it goes back to being a sharefish. Those people with the closed jars had experienced God in some form but either weren't going to share it with anyone or at least not with anyone who wasn't like them, right?"

"Right. I've about exhausted this water imagery, but let me take it one step further to illustrate a point. Some people who get close to experiencing God get scared because they know that to truly experience God they have to give up being the focal point of their own lives. They just can't do it so they walk around showing everyone they know what God is about. They just keep a lid on Him. Other folks have experienced God but because they are so focused on themselves they don't even realize it, like the folks who are walking through the puddles without knowing it. Believe it or not there are even those who are shown the way down the path but choose not to go even though their very souls urge them to. Only those who have opened themselves to experiencing God's full magnificence share that experience with everyone they meet, hoping that they too will want to feel what they feel."

I scratched my head. "Ok, Izzy, I get it. I think I really get it. I...I just...."

"What?" Izzy's eyes were still moist from the power of his story.

"Where does Jesus fit into all this?" I finally blurted out, ashamed I didn't know.

Izzy reached over and put his hand on my shoulder. He smiled from the depths of his soul and a lone tear tenderly slid down his weathered cheek as he softly replied. "Who do you think guided *me* down that path?"

Chapter 18

An Open Heart

We both just stared out the windshield for about an hour after we left the diner. The silence was comfortable, almost reverent. I kept going over my days with Izzy in my mind again and again. He had shared so many nuggets of wisdom that I wanted to make sure I remembered them all:

"If you have to tell people you are humble, you aren't."

"God made you to be the best *you*. The good news is that He wants to help you do it."

"Ask God to help you stay out of His way, and discover the amazing things about this life He wants to show you."

"God made us in His image for a reason. Pray for that reason."

"People may forget what you say. People may forget what you do. People will ALWAYS remember how you make them feel."

The list was so vast yet so powerful. My favorite was something that Izzy said he had read a long time ago in a work by theologian Howard Thurman: "Don't ask what the world needs. Ask instead what makes you come alive. Go and do that; for what the world needs is more people who have come alive." He had gone through so much, yet through it all had emerged with an amazing clarity of purpose. I wondered what would have happened to me if I had experienced what Izzy did. I quickly stopped myself. "It's not a race. Not a competition. Each of us is a unique creation of God," I told myself. I couldn't help but grin at my reflection in the windshield. What an epiphany. I had changed.

I realized for the first time that for my entire life I had always compared myself unfavorably to people around me. I had always told myself that I was not as "whatever" as the other person was. I would argue with my Dad because I told myself I wasn't good enough to be loved by him. I disrespected my Mom because I knew I had disappointed her time and time again and was not worthy of her trust. Could it really be possible that God had made me special and had a special plan just for me? Could this be what I have been searching for all my life?

Even though I still had many questions, I felt clarity of purpose. Rather, I felt clarity that I HAD a purpose and for once the fact that I didn't exactly know what that was, was OK. I didn't even know what to do next. An excitement burned in my soul. Before I could really even think about it, I found myself praying silently to God - the same almighty God in whom only days before I had questioned my belief and most certainly had no concept of His belief in me.

I asked for forgiveness for all the times I had led a selfish life. I asked for guidance in living more of a sharefish life. I asked for patience as I continued to question things like where I was spiritually, who He was, and where He wanted me to go and what he wanted me to do. I prayed for help in finding what makes me "come alive" so I could go and do it. I thanked Him for everyone in my life who had not given up on me, who I knew still loved me even though I had continued to make errors in judgment. I thanked him for Izzy and for Jesus, for my folks and grandparents, and for my close friends who had remained my friends even when I didn't treat them fairly.

I know it was only a few minutes, but it felt like I had prayed for hours. As I closed my prayer, I asked God to please help me to stay out of his way as he and I grew closer together. When I silently said "Amen," I could have sworn I heard Izzy say it softly as well. Exhausted, I fell into a deep, refreshing, dreamless sleep.

Chapter 19

Welcome to North Carolina

I was startled by hearing my name and feeling a poke in the ribs. "Nyles! Wake up!" It was Izzy, grinning from ear to ear. "I've been sitting here on the side of the road waiting for you to wake up for about twenty minutes. I thought you'd want to see this." Izzy pointed out over the dashboard of his truck straight down the road. I rubbed my eyes and squinted through the bug-splattered windshield. The "Welcome to North Carolina" sign shone brightly in the headlights, the reflective paint used for the letters making the message almost jump off the sign. I smiled, then laughed. For the first time I could remember, seeing that sign gave me hope instead of dread. It excited me instead of depressing me. The road ahead cut a ribbon through the Great Smoky Mountains like a familiar path. In the peaceful glow of the moon on this cloudless night the huge hardwood and evergreen trees that lined the highway seemed to welcome me with luminescent open arms. I smiled as I imagined their tree cousins in Oregon who had waved me good luck at the start of this incredible journey somehow had sent word I was on my way. I couldn't wait to get home.

We stopped and ate at another diner (where did Izzy find these places?) and I regaled him with stories of my family and the places we had lived. I talked about my friends and how surprised they were going to be to see me. One thing was kind of strange. We didn't discuss my newfound energy in the Spirit, although Izzy's eyes danced like never before as he listened to me until almost midnight. Exhaustion finally wrestled my excitement and won. Sensing this, Izzy yawned and said, "I'll think I'll turn in. I'll see you in a few hours, Nyles." Izzy once again slept in his truck and I slept in the clean but inexpensive hotel that shared the parking lot with the diner.

Early the next morning we ate breakfast and headed east on Highway 40. Around lunchtime, we drove up to the grocery store that had stood at that familiar corner for 80 years. It was only two blocks from my house and it made it easy for Izzy to negotiate his truck in and out.

I hopped out and met Izzy around the front of the truck. He tossed my bag to me and reached out his hand. I grabbed his hand, dropped my bag and surprised myself by giving him a bear hug.

"I don't know how to thank you," I stammered. Izzy just dropped his head back and laughed a hearty laugh. "You already have, my friend...and you will even more." Before I could invite him to meet my folks, he had jumped back in the driver's seat, blew the horn a couple of times, and lumbered down the road to get back on the highway. I stood there in the parking lot of the grocery store, watching the truck as it got smaller and smaller until it disappeared over a rise. I grabbed my bag and headed down the sidewalk to my folks' house. On the way the specter of the last time I was there invaded my mind and sent a chill of apprehension to my soul. I had yelled at Mom and Dad and told them I hated them and never wanted to see them again. I had slammed the door on my way out vowing never to return. It had been five years. My selfish side tried to talk me out of going back. "What did I need them for?" my selfish side asked. It pointed out all the times my folks didn't agree with what I wanted to do. I slowed as the selfish side began to take over.

Then I began to pray.

"I don't know what you want from me, God. I know you and I have a lot of catching up to do. Right now, though, I need two things. I need courage and I need you to help me get out of your way. Please help me be a sharefish."

My pace slowly picked back up and the selfish thoughts began to fade like ghosts in the cool fall breeze. As soon as I passed the big elm and the hedgerow of the Murphy's house, I saw it. Home. I stopped for a few minutes to take it all in. Memories began to flood my mind. I took a deep breath, said another silent prayer for strength, and walked down the sidewalk where I had learned to ride my bike, ducked under the low branch of the elm tree that Dad had tied a blue ribbon around when I was born, and stopped in my tracks. There on the porch were my Mom and Dad. In a split second that seemed like an hour, my life ran through my mind like the highlights of a bad movie. "What would their reaction be to me coming home after the way I had left?" I wondered.

My answer came swiftly. With hands waving high and smiles on their faces they ran across the yard and hugged me. Sensing the puzzled look on my face, my Mom wiped away a tear and told me that Mr. Murphy had called them when he saw me walking in front of his house. They couldn't believe it. I was having trouble maintaining composure with all the emotions I was feeling. Relief. Regret. Thankfulness. Embarrassment. There was so much to say I didn't know where to begin.

Of course, my Mom knew exactly where to begin. At the kitchen table. In between her fried chicken and green beans and real mashed potatoes and her wonderful sweet tea I told them all about my Pacific coast experiences. When I started telling them about Izzy and our trip across the country, they both stared at me with their jaws dropped, with an occasional "can you believe what you're hearing?" look passing between them. They didn't even ask me what a sharefish was when I first mentioned it. I have to admit, it wasn't the first time my folks didn't know what to say when they were listening to one of my stories, but it was the first time I felt wonderful telling it.

I apologized for my behavior the last time I was at home. We talked about it for a while and I realized that I had some work to do to get my relationship with them to the point it needed to be. I laughed when I realized that it was the same way with my relationship with God. When my Dad asked what was so funny, I surprised my folks and myself by actually being honest with my feelings. I told them from the heart how I was building my relationship with God.

"Son," my Dad said softly while putting his hand on mine, "Your mother and I prayed for you every day you were gone, and just like God our love for you is just as strong as ever." Tears streaked his face as he clutched my hand. "I love you too," I said. I quickly wondered if I had ever told him that but just as quickly told myself that the past didn't matter. Boy, I HAD changed. We hugged again as my Mom brought out some of her famous peach cobbler, which reminded me of the peach pie I had at the diner before I met Izzy. It seemed like a lifetime ago. Today was the happiest day of my life.

Chapter 20

New Beginnings

Word quickly spread throughout the family that I had come home. My sister and brother and their families came to the house within the next two weeks and wanted to hear my story. My nieces loved the sharefish story, and to my brother and sister's surprise, actively strived to be more like sharefish. Whenever one of them would act self-centered the other would say, "It's better to be a sharefish than a selfish!" Then they would both laugh and move on. My nephew was captivated by Izzy and kept asking questions about him. I had few answers. I realized that even though he changed my life and had shared with me his gut-wrenching story, I didn't really know that much about him.

I tried to reconnect with him but could not find his trucking company anywhere. I actually traveled one day to the last diner where we stopped but it was out of business and strangely looked like it had been for quite a while. I often wished I could talk to him and let him know how much I appreciated his friendship and discuss with him the impact he had on my life.

I got a job at a local cabinet shop and lived at home until I could get back on my feet a bit financially. It was a time of renewed relationships with my Mom and especially my Dad. We would sit on the porch after dinner and I would ask him things about the Bible or about faith in general. At first, I would just listen to what he said. I would then do some research and reading to clarify what we had discussed. Eventually, I surprised us both by actually bringing up some insightful points of my own. We would laugh and talk and debate and question and pray until late in the night.

It took a great deal of effort to be a sharefish at first. My selfish side would rear its ugly head whenever my folks would say something that reminded me of the old days. I would have to say a quick prayer and ask God to help me get out of His way. Old friends who tempted me with the lifestyle that I used to revel in laughed at me and my new attitude toward life and began to ignore me. Friends of our family who I had always thought were God-fearing people actually acted like they were afraid of me. They would avoid me in church and the scuttlebutt was that they didn't believe I had actually changed at all. Izzy was right about people. I had to dig hard some days.

Day by day, things became a little easier. I would falter a bit, get up, dust off my spirit and bruised ego, ask for forgiveness, and keep on going. In time, people got used to me and I got fewer and fewer raised eyebrows when I would chaperone the youth group at church or lead a devotional small group. I told my story over and over and each time I told it, it sunk in a little deeper. The more I realized that I was unworthy of God's love, the more loved I felt by Him. The more I gave in His name, the more I received. The less I compared myself to other people, the better I felt about myself. The more I shared, the less I thought about myself. Just like Izzy said, the dark side knew my weaknesses and would whisper in my ear. Sometimes I could resist, sometimes I did not. God was always there to love me either way.

The sharefish life began as something I had to fight to do. The selfish in me was deeply rooted. Izzy told me that whenever I needed help becoming who God wanted me to be, I should pray that God would give me fertilizer for the things that He wanted to grow inside me, and the strength to starve those things He wanted to shrivel and die within me.

As I matured in my faith, I began to pray for someone with whom to share my life and faith. I felt that I was ready, and had read that God wants us to come to Him with every desire of our heart, so I figured it was worth a try. I had gone to several functions and had met some really nice ladies, but no one really spoke to the deepest areas of my heart. I began to feel a little depressed about it. The roots of doubt began to take hold of my spirit. Was I praying too little? Too much? Should I be praying about this at all?

Little did I know that God had something very special planned for me. One day I was helping a friend take care of his dogs while he was out of town. His neighbors came by when I was walking them and we quickly became friends. As it turns out, a very dear friend of theirs had just moved to town from Florida and they wondered if I would be interested in meeting her.

I was and we did.

Her name was Rebecca and she was beautiful inside and out. We became friends and both knew that something special had happened when we met. A few short weeks later we began seeing each other. One day, we went for a long walk down miles of trails cut through a stately hardwood forest in a local state park. The sun cut ribbons of light through the canopy of leaves and branches that waved a cool breeze around us as we walked. Nervously, I told her my story. I didn't want things to go too far without her knowing exactly what she was getting into.

She listened. I mean, really listened. She would nod occasionally and ask a question, and I could tell she knew how important it was for me to open my heart to her. When we finished our walk, I don't know if it was the trail or my emotions, but I was exhausted. I sat on a log, took a deep breath, and let out a long slow sigh. As I stared at the ribbons of sunlight I realized that I had been more open with Rebecca in the short time that I had known her than with anyone I had ever met.

When I turned to thank her for listening, our eyes met and the eternal question that had been buzzing in my soul was answered. I had found my sharefish soul mate.

A few months later, a Godwink happened. A Godwink is when something happens to you that tickles your spirit and you know that God is grinning at you when it happens, something that a cynic may call coincidence.

I knew better.

Chapter 21

Keep the Faith

A group from the church I had joined decided to go on a mission trip. A couple of missionaries who had ties to our church had begun an initiative in one of the poorest counties in the country. This initiative was to plant seeds of forgiveness between races, plant seeds of hope for the people of the community, and plant seeds of faith for the people who did not know God. It sounded like a perfect place to practice being a sharefish. When they announced the location of this trip, I thought my jaw would hit the floor.

Johnsonville, Arkansas. The same place that Izzy had gone with his church. What a Godwink!

As we made our plans, I wondered if I would meet Sammy Blues Jones or his son Michael. I was excited. I became more excited when Rebecca decided to cancel a trip to a conference at Martha's Vineyard in Massachusetts so she could go on the mission trip. "What a sharefish," I thought to myself.

We crossed over the Mississippi River into Johnsonville, Arkansas in the middle of an afternoon in mid-June. The temperature and humidity both hovered around triple digits. Abandoned buildings with broken windows and boarded up doors lined the streets like a war zone. We passed a small group of people sitting in tattered lawn chairs in the shade of a large maple tree in the courtyard of a dilapidated public housing complex. They eyed the bus suspiciously as we stopped at the four-way stop on our way through town.

Our group was a bit nervous but full of hope as we began to get to know the people in the community. The effect of the missionaries there was evident almost immediately. People from different races, different faiths, different socio-economic situations, different educational levels, different backgrounds, and different aspirations, all came together in the Spirit. It was a truly remarkable sharefish experience that can be summarized in one event. On Wednesday night one of the local churches hosted a service that featured church leaders from both black and white congregations in the community, the first such event in the city's history.

The church was packed. For one night all was forgiven, no one was judged, and all were brothers and sisters. The gospel music awakened our souls like a rooster at sunrise. The ministers stirred our faith and charged our spirits with energy and passion. We rocked the house. I looked over at Rebecca and she beamed.

We were still riding high on the previous night's experience when we began our third day of baseball camp the next morning. As the twenty boys between the ages of eight and ten came running across the field from their bible school lesson, I was eager to convey the spirit of mutual respect and spiritual excitement I had enjoyed the night before.

Then I saw Obed. My heart sank a little. Obed was a bright-eyed intelligent eight-year old. He was smaller than most of the other boys but made up for it in his unbridled spirit. He also had an uncanny ability to find trouble. He had been disciplined by the instructors in just about every group during the week. I prayed for guidance and strength.

After teams had been chosen and sent to the dugouts, we prepared to play our practice game. A commotion broke out in one of the dugouts. Obed had gotten into a scuffle with one of the ten year olds. After pulling them apart, I took Obed over to the side of the dugout and knelt down so we were eye to eye. He looked at me defiantly, ready to defend his actions.

I looked at him intently. I wasn't sure what to say, but knew I had to reach this boy somehow. For some reason I can't explain, I felt led to tell him that I needed him to do a special job for me. His eyes immediately changed from defiance to curiosity. I explained that I need someone to take charge of his team and to assign each player a position and to put together a batting order. I asked him if he thought he could handle the responsibility.

His eyes got wide and he nodded excitedly. He shocked me by saying an enthusiastic "Yes, sir, coach!" I went back over to the dugout and explained to the boys what Obed was going to do. There were a few murmurs and chuckles, but no objections. To my surprise, that boy had everyone sitting on the bench in batting order in just a few minutes! Obed ran back to me. 'All done, coach!' he said excitedly. I knelt down again and thanked him and told him he had done a great job. I held out my hand. He gave me a high five and ran back to the dugout.

We began the game and I kept wondering what in the world had gotten into Obed to change him so dramatically. My concentration was snapped by shouts that were coming from the other dugout. It looked like another fight. I ran over to see what was going on. There was Obed, surrounded by boys. "That didn't last long," I said to myself. As I approached the dugout, Obed saw me and came running. "I'm getting the other team straight too!" he grinned. I laughed and patted him on the head.

We had a great game. When the horn blew to signal lunchtime, the boys took off across the field to get their bag lunches. I began to pick up the equipment when Obed came running up to me. "Need some help, coach?" he asked. I smiled and nodded.

Later that evening I talked with the missionaries about Obed and his family. After hearing the story, I understood why Obed was so disruptive. Obed had unwittingly witnessed a brutal murder a couple of years earlier. He watched in horror as someone was shot ten times at point blank range. He was six years old at the time.

I felt the urge to talk with Obed further. The next day I asked Obed if I could eat lunch with him. We sat under a tree with our bag lunches and talked about the week and what his favorite things were in the camp. When I felt the timing was right, I began to tell him that I saw some awesome leadership qualities in him. I explained that leaders are very rare and that both the good guys and the bad guys need them. I looked at him squarely and told him that he had the choice of which side he was going to lead. I grabbed his shoulders and softly but firmly told him that God needs good leaders. He thought for awhile as he chewed his peanut butter and jelly sandwich. He took a long drink of lemonade and then looked at me deeply and said, "I want to be a leader for the *good* guys, coach."

I went to the dugout and got my backpack. I came back over to Obed. I reached in and got my Bible. I asked him if he knew what it was. He nodded. I asked him if he had one. He shook his head. I handed mine to him and told him that it would teach him everything he needed to know about being a good leader. I told him if he studied hard in school and read his Bible that he could be whatever he wanted to be when he grew up. "Even a pro basketball player or the President?" he asked. I nodded and laughed. I told him that if that was what God wanted him to be, then his job was to be the best one he could be. Basketball player, or President.

From that point on, Obed was my buddy. Whenever we had group activities he would find Rebecca and me and sit with us. I met his mother and grandmother and we became fast friends. He still had his high energy level, but the fights and disruptions ended.

A man from the mission board came by the baseball field the next day with a video camera. He was filming highlights of the camp and had heard about Obed and me. He wanted to do a short interview. As he set up his camera, I found Obed and asked him if he wanted to be filmed talking with me. "I'm gonna be on TV!" Obed shouted to everyone as he raced across the baseball field toward the man with the camera.

I was not prepared for what happened during the interview. I knelt beside Obed as the man began filming. The man asked Obed about the camp and what he had learned so far. Obed put his arm around me and said that the color of a person's skin didn't matter to him any more. He said that God loved us all and that was all that mattered. He said that he and I were going to be best buddies forever. He was right.

That Christmas a small package arrived for me. It was from Obed.

I opened the package. There was a small item wrapped in newspaper and an envelope. On the front of the envelope were the words "to Coach." Inside the envelope was a folded up piece of paper. I pulled the paper out. It was a card made out of a piece of notebook paper with the torn edge carefully cut off. On the front was a crayon drawing of two stick figures playing baseball. Both had big smiles. Across the top in big letters it said "KEEP THE FAITH." I began to read out loud:

Dear Coach,

   It was great meeting you this summer. Thank you for being my friend and for teaching us baseball. Thank you for giving me your baseball glove too. It helps me catch good. I wanted to tell you that I just got into a special school here that will help me be the leader you said I can be. I will study hard and do good. You keep telling me to keep the faith and I am. I read the Bible you gave me every day and even sometimes read it to my sister. I saw this wristband at the store and had to buy it for you for Christmas.

Keeping the Faith

Obed

   I was grinning through the tears. I lifted my right sleeve and put on the multicolored wristband. Embossed in it were the words "KEEP THE FAITH."

   Awesome.

Chapter 22

Now!

The next day we were clearing a vacant lot in a blighted area downtown so we could plant a vegetable garden for the local people. Groups of the city's skeptics and curious eyed us suspiciously from corners and abandoned buildings as we worked to dig out brick fragments from the soil.

About mid-afternoon I took a break and glanced over at Rebecca. Her blue shirt was turning different hues from the perspiration spots, her pants were covered in brick dust, her oversized gardening hat which was protecting her from sunburn but not from the heat was slightly cocked on her head from constant bending to pick up bricks, and her face had dirt marks where she would wipe sweat from dripping. She was beautiful.

I suddenly was overcome by a feeling. I would love to say that it was the voice of God, but I didn't really *hear* anything. I just felt it. One word. "Now." "Now?" I asked. Again, just the one word. "Now." Even though I had not planned it, I knew exactly what to do. I put down my rake and asked her if she would like to take a break and go for a walk up the block to the river. There, on the banks of the Mississippi River, in the middle of the heat, both of us dirty, smelly, and exhausted, I asked her to marry me. I don't know if it was the heat or the exhaust fumes from the trucks loading the barges, but she said yes.

We walked back to the work site and our minister looked up and joked "Where'd you two run off to? Did you get engaged or something?" We laughed and said that's exactly what happened. Everyone stopped what they were doing and crowded around us and congratulated us. The dirt and perspiration did not slow down the hugs. Even the local people came to congratulate us, including one of our new friends; Mrs. Bullard from Bullard's Home Cooking, a restaurant and pool hall across the street from our worksite. Mrs. Bullard sat in her plastic chair in the shade, keeping an eye on us and our progress while providing security for our supplies when we would leave the site. She was the matriarch of the community and having her support for our project was key to its success.

Since this was an unplanned event, there was one thing missing to make it all official. A ring. In short order a group of folks quickly fashioned a ten-penny nail into a ring. As I slipped it on her finger, the crowd cheered like they were at the Super Bowl. It was amazing how quickly a simple inexpensive nail can suddenly become priceless.

We all decided to celebrate by walking across the street to Mrs. Bullard's for an early supper. As we approached the restaurant, I stopped in my tracks as I heard familiar laughter coming from inside. "It can't be," I said to myself as I shook my head. I pushed open the screen door and as my eyes refocused from the bright sunshine to the dim neon lights, there in the corner sitting with a couple of old locals was Izzy.

I rushed in and when he saw me he grinned from ear to ear and gave me a big hug. Later I would reflect that he didn't seem surprised to see me, but I was so overwhelmed by the events of the day I couldn't think straight. I formally introduced him to everyone. I say *formally* because everyone already had heard about my cross-country adventure with Izzy. I then introduced Rebecca to Izzy. It was as though they had always known each other. Our group shared a wonderful meal of fried chicken, pork chops, turnip greens, mashed potatoes, sweet corn, homemade biscuits and gravy, and peach cobbler for dessert that would almost bring you to tears.

As we were leaving, I hugged Izzy again and told him how much I appreciated all he had done for me. His eyes danced and he laughed and said he didn't do anything but tell me how to get out of God's way. He waved good-bye to Mrs. Bullard and left. As the screen door of the restaurant slammed shut, I remembered that once again I had neglected to get his address or phone number. I asked Mrs. Bullard if she had it, but she just shook her head. I bolted out the door to catch him. He was nowhere to be found.

Chapter 23

Paying It Forward

As the years passed, being a sharefish took less thought but just as much determination. The world was always right there in my face, tempting me with newer and better things "guaranteed" to make me feel newer and better. I felt an even deeper kinship to my friend John because I now understood the all-consuming power of being addicted to something. I realized that for years I had been addicted to *me*. The world was partly responsible but I was *accountable*. Going through spiritual "rehab" had gotten me on a clearer path, but the talons of the "me" addiction were always ready to dig their steely claws into my head. The relapses were frequent and blatant at first and the tag team of Guilt and Pride were always in the wings ready to be my best friends once again. Just like John, I gathered strength by surrounding myself with as many "sponsors" as I could.

I soon realized that no day would ever pass without a relapse of some sort because I was hopelessly human, but God was always there to love me and encourage me to keep trying. That nugget of truth helped me grow every day and gave me strength.

I got more involved in things that would strengthen the sharefish side of my life. I found that I got great pleasure from mission trips and spending time with those who were going through tough times or had been forgotten in our society. I took advantage of every opportunity I had to spend time doing both. It was incredibly uplifting to hear the stories these people told of unbelievable obstacles that they had experienced but were now overcoming through their faith and hope.

In other cases, when the people would be at the end of their physical and spiritual ropes, I would pray that our dialogue would help give them the strength to persevere and to grow. In all cases, setting aside the selfish trait of comparison and embracing the sharefish way of life blessed me greatly. Above it all, being a sharefish forces me to mature spiritually in a way I would have thought impossible before. I have to admit, though, that sometimes it happens in spite of me instead of because of me.

I didn't have to go on an organized mission trip or spend time with the marginalized in our society to reap the benefits of being a sharefish. Examples of this newfound sharefish energy began to show up in my everyday life. To the obviously unmotivated person in the drive-through window at the fast food restaurant and the person who cut me off in traffic I was able to have a more patient spirit. My business relationships reflected my beliefs and I soon discovered and was pleasantly surprised how much less stressful my working life became.

My relationships with my friends and family improved because I began to *truly listen* to what they were saying instead of waiting for them to take a breath so I could impress them with how much I knew about the topic. I didn't know it, but I was becoming who God had always wanted me to be. It was the most amazing feeling in the world. I felt significant. I felt loved. I felt appreciated. I felt I was part of something bigger than me. And the best part was I felt these things from a place inside of me that no human had ever been able to reach. I was getting right with God.

One Sunday I was invited to a local church to tell them my story. Many kind people came up to me afterward and told me that they were going to focus on being sharefish. I looked at each one as they shook my hand or hugged me and silently prayed for God to give them the strength He had given me.

As I was talking to a woman with a particularly large pink hat, I heard a familiar laugh behind her in the crowd. Her hat made it impossible for me to see anything behind her without being rude.

As she moved away, I craned my neck to see if it was possible...Yes! There he was. Izzy. He waved and smiled and waited his turn. I wondered how he could have known that I was speaking there that day. I have to admit that I found myself hurrying people along a bit so I could see him. It seemed that everyone wanted to talk too long, or had questions. I had to dig very deep to stay connected with each and every one. It took everything I had to be a sharefish!

His turn finally came. We hugged long and hard. "I'm very proud of you, Nyles," he said. I told him how thankful I was to have met him and how much he had changed my life. His eyes danced their familiar dance as he said, "All I did was help you to become yourself." I told him about how I am reminded of him each and every day. "Really? How so?" he asked with a puzzled look.

Startled by a noise behind him, he turned just in time to see a beautiful five-year old girl pick up a pocketbook that had been dropped on the floor by an elderly woman sitting in the first row. After handing the flustered woman her pocketbook, the little girl announced, "Don't worry. I like helping people. Now it's your turn to help someone else! You keep your eyes open, 'kay? My daddy says you always have to be ready to be a sharefish, and it's better to be a sharefish than a selfish!" The woman laughed.

The little girl then kissed the smiling woman on the cheek and darted away. Catching my eye, she came running up to the two of us, her dark curls bouncing around her face and her smile showing her recently lost tooth in the bottom front. "Daddy! Daddy!" she screamed as she jumped into my arms, grabbed me around the neck, and planted a big kiss on *my* cheek.

"I would like for you to meet, my daughter," I said to my friend as I fought back tears. "Tell him your name sweetheart," I said.

"My name is Isabella Grace," she said with her angel's voice. She then leaned over to him and whispered, "My friends call me Izzy."

Do you have a sharefish story?

Share your sharefish story with the world at

www.sharefish.org

Come in for a visit. Read sharefish stories from people just like you, share your own story with everyone, and help spread the sharefish message.

Show the world you are a sharefish! Order your sharefish sticker when you visit www.sharefish.org.

Acknowledgements

This story was originally written for my son, Oren. Shortly after we found out Becky was pregnant in the spring of 2007, I started this story and it was a race to finish it before he was born. He won. I hope one day when he is older and out of his diapers he will read this and it will help him understand life (and maybe his dad) a little better.

Wow. Having a child is the ultimate definition of unconditional love. If God truly loves us as His children, and I believe He does, we will be OK.

It is wonderful to be blessed with family and friends. My wife Becky is one of the most amazing people you could ever meet. How I convinced her to marry me I'll never know. It's a prime example of the power of prayer!

My parents' gift to me was that I always knew they loved me and were always there for me. My mission is that my wife and son will always be able to say that about me. My two sisters, Donna and Lynne, have always been much more than family to me. They have been wonderful friends my entire life as well. My brother, O.R., has shown me that time and distance are not inhibitors of love and devotion. Becky's mom, Joyce, has been a great source of encouragement and prayer for this story. Thank you, Mama Joyce!

The blessings of friendship of Chuck, Jeremy and Moe (who are just like brothers to me) have affected me more than they will ever know. My new hermano en Cristo Ben will always have a special place in my heart for allowing me to be a part of his life-changing spiritual immersion. The rest of my Honduran mission teams have given me more spiritual energy than they will ever know and are outstanding examples of how sharefish have no borders. They, and an especially inspirational ambassador for Christ, Ricardo, and his devotion to his life's calling, Mercy and Grace Ministries (www.mercyandgraceministries.org), are an inspiration to me and are on my prayer list each night. We are because He is!

The folks at North Carolina Baptist Men also continue to amaze me at how organized they are when sending teams to wherever help is needed. Dios te Ama! My Arkansas Mission teams at First Baptist Church through the years have been an incredible sharefish example to the Mississippi Delta and the friendships I have developed with the wonderful people of "Johnsonville" are priceless to me. Keep the Faith, Debo!

Quantum thanks to friends like Martin who helped me to finally understand myself and what I'm supposed to do with my life and to Bob and Julie who have given untold time, encouragement and resources to help me get the www.sharefish.org message started. Other friends who are like family like Jeff and Bob and Jeremiah and Sam and Steve and Mark will never know how much they mean to me, which is probably a good thing because it would go straight to their heads (just kidding). Seriously, though, whenever I have a crazy thought I know I can go to them without worry of prejudice or consternation.

I offer deep gratitude to dear friends like Debbie, Mallory and Michelle, who, along with others, read the story as it developed and gave wonderful insight and support.

The Formations Class, the Sons of Thunder, the Band of Brothers, the staff of First Baptist Church of Raleigh, and members like Dr. Elmo Scoggin have always been indefatigable sources for history of religion, faith perspectives and historical text translation. Wow. Talk about spiritual fertilizer! You are awesome!

I have read so much John Ortberg, Philip Yancey, C.S. Lewis, Donald Miller, Kenneth Bailey, Franklin Graham, Tony Campolo, T. D. Jakes, Beth Moore, Max Lucado, Lee Strobel, Brian McLaren, John Eldridge, and Bruce Feiler through the years that I feel that they are personal spiritual coaches to me. My utmost gratitude to them all for sharing their literary gifts with everyone.

To a special woman, Miss Murk, my high school English teacher, thank you - for all the years of believing in your students and for helping them believe in themselves.

To you, the reader, who for some reason picked this story out of the millions you could have chosen, I sincerely thank you. A Godwink, perhaps? I hope the story spoke to you and that you will be blessed by something in it and inspired to lead a sharefish life. If so, I pray that God will give you the strength and courage to find out how amazing it is. When you do, make sure to come to www.sharefish.org and tell us about your experiences!

Most graciously I thank God for keeping me out of His way and giving me the strength to put this story on paper.

3219785

Made in the USA